Cast a Long Shadow

2nd Edition

By Jim Banks

Also author of;

Introduction

Each of us has a built-in desire to make our lives count. It was built-in by God so that our lives would be beneficial to those around us and through our efforts the world would be a better place for those coming behind us. There are as many variations in how this is achieved as there are different people. In spite of all that wars against us, we were created for a whole host of positive contributions. It is entirely up to us how great a mark we wish to make on our local circles, society in general, or the world at large.

As for me, I have never been one to want to impact the entire world, but in some small measure that's what has happened with the advent of the Trauma Prayer that was recorded in 2009. I was simply trying to solve a problem for a dozen young ladies back in 2008, but apparently the Lord had something bigger in mind. The audio version of that prayer found on Youtube, Vimeo and our website has found its way via the internet and CD's copied by the thousands into every country in the world by what by now may be as many as 2,000,000 people. We guess that at as many as 20,000 folks got to sleep to it every night.

The title of *Cast A Long Shadow* came to me as I was approaching the anniversary of my 70th birthday and spending a little time considering how I might spend the balance of my years. The original thought was, "I wonder how many good years I have left?" By "good years" I meant that I would have the health and energy to do what I felt the Lord had for me to do. Then my next thought was, "How will I spend them to make the greatest impact?" My thoughts drifted off to how many people could I possibly touch and what mechanism could I use. You know the drill ... All the calculating and postulating that we humans do when faced with a potential opportunity. Call it dreaming. At the time, I was sitting out under a tree in Mozambique waiting for Pat to finish dressing for the day. She came out to begin our assigned activities and my musing ceased.

The next morning found me outside under that same tree awaiting Pat again, when I was surprised by the Lord asking me, *"How many good years do you want?"* I have to say, that was a bit of a shock, but in hind sight I shouldn't have been so shocked for it seemed that a number of Biblical heroes found themselves drawn into bargaining with God; Moses and Abraham to name just two. MY y reply was 20 years. He said, "How about 15?" To this day I don't know why I didn't start with a higher number. So there I was having one of the two original questions answered, but what of the second?

In my mind that's the initial direction of our lives is pretty much up to each of us to determine, but is certainly subject to interruption and redirection. The content of these two verses is actually what is responsible for setting the course;

> Psalms 37:23 *"The steps of a good man are ordered by the LORD: and he delighteth in his way."*
> Proverbs 16:9 *"A man's heart deviseth (plans) his way: but the LORD directeth (orders) his steps."*

The idea is that you and I cannot see as the Lord does. He sees the end from the beginning, while you and I only dream of the end and must plan a step or two to begin. It's rather like the rudder of a ship. The rudder is useless if the ship is not moving, but it easily changes the course of the ship once there is forward motion. So let the dreaming begin!

For me, the course was set back in 1983 or 84 when we prayed a prayer (or perhaps more accurately, made a declaration before the Lord) the results of which prophesied no relevant ideas about what would eventually be require of us; *"If you will teach us how to fix broken people we will give our lives to it."* Now, I have to warn you about praying such prayers or making such declarations , for you (like us) have no idea the price that it is going to exact.

What we had in mind was simply a three or four day seminar – a week long one tops – and then we'll be good to go; never intending (nor suspecting) that it would become a full time, life-long learning venture. All we knew at the time was that those around us that we cared for, we were seemingly powerless to help get to the next level. Yes, we picked them up, dusted them off, applied a bandaid to a scrape, patted them on the butt and sent them back out into the fray, only to have to repeat the process again soon thereafter. I'm not sure what you call that, but it sure wasn't healing. The Lord apparently had other ideas.

Since those days we have prayed over, taught, mentored and instructed thousands. Nice job! You might say, but none of us is ever really satisfied with what is in the rear view mirror, for the challenge is always before us. There is no all-fulfilling destination in this life – the joy is in the journey. So the idea of looking at my 70th birthday was one of "what's next?" and thinking about how I would like to spend the remainder of my working life.

Just so you'll know, retirement is not a Biblical concept. We spent 3 ½ years in the golf business in the late 90's and we joke that we prayed for more people then by accident than we do now on purpose. We are who we are and that's what we'll always do. So retirement is like saying I'm going to become somebody else when I get old. That's stupid.

The other thing about 'retirement' is that people have the American ideal firmly planted in their minds that one day I'll get to do what I want to do, rather than having to do this. That thinking (or perhaps the assumption that this is the way it all works) keeps your future – and the sense of personal fulfillment - 'out there' somewhere …

out of reach until you get to a certain age or feel you that have the financial resources to engage it. That too is stupid.

There are those ordinal birthdays when it is time to review where you are in life and where you would like to be by the end of the next phase. For many it's 21, 30, 50, or 60. My biggie was actually at 55. It was at that point that I decided that I had had enough of secular livelihood and decided to pursue advancing the Kingdom of God full time. But even at 55 years of age, I never took one minute to consider what life might look like at 70 and how I would want to spend the following years. I was too busy dealing with day-to-day issues. I had never thought of ministering internationally. I had never stopped to consider what Continent I might be on when ministering. It just sorta snuck up on us. In the last five years alone we have been to England, Scotland, Germany, Holland, Mozambique, South Africa, Jordan, Israel, The Philippines and Thailand – many of them several times. During that time we have put our toes in the Atlantic, the North Sea, the Caribbean, the Pacific, the South Pacific, the Dead Sea, the South China Sea and the Indian Ocean.

So…. Why this book?

Looking into the future of my remaining work/ministry years caused me to think about other Biblical characters and how they closed out their work/ministry lives and what we find is a whole series of failures. In fact, very few Biblical individuals finished very well. The obvious question was, "Why not?" and the answer seemed to be one of two reasons; either they didn't really understand and adhere to the mandates of the Kingdom of God, or they had never created the habits and corresponding heart attitudes that would guide them well into their declining years. That's two books. This one, and the next, *Finishing Well* (also available on Amazom.com.)

My premise is that the direction noted in the next to last verse of Matthew Chapter 6 is a significant life key for believers; "*seek first*

the Kingdom of God and His righteousness." If we will but make an effort to understand the precepts and principles of the Kingdom of God then we can make the choices necessary, not only to finish well, but see to it that our lives will cast a long shadow for the stature that we attain will impact thousands, for generations to come.

1   Pay Close Attention ...

It is indeed strange how the Lord captures our attention about a specific subject that is central to His heart. I wrote a book entitled *"The Insidious Dance; The Paralysis of Perfectionism"* back in 2013 and although it was intended to strike deeply at the heart of a specific malady that many of my clients (for prayer ministry; inner healing and deliverance) were experiencing the fallout of, I never suspected that it would also be the crowbar the Lord would use to really open my eyes to the Kingdom of God, or the Kingdom of Heaven. But He is well able to use anything at His disposal to bring you to a more mature place in Him. The fact that I had been struggling to exit the remnants of perfectionism for several years gave me some valued additional insight into the real source of the problem, as well as its ramifications in my relationships, particularly with Him.

Up until this point I was a great believer in the reality of "positional theology." I grew up, as did my parents and grandparents, in the traditions of the Southern Baptist Denomination, which was predominately about salvation. In spite of that fact that I had no concrete idea of what I had done or what it would mean, I accepted Jesus Christ as my Savior and Lord, and I asked Him to come into my life and run the show at the ripe old age of 9. I was Baptized in a little church in Opelousas, Louisiana and later (like 25 years later) I was 'filled with the Spirit' listening to a radio program in Indianapolis, Indiana while in my car during the lunch hour. Up to that point the totality of my understanding of salvation and baptism was that I had received my "Get Out Of Hell Free Card" and I was now a citizen of the Kingdom of God, sealed somehow by the stamp of Holy Spirit upon me. That's the savior part of the equation. Positionally, all of that was and is true. When you're in, you're in. But there's a bit more to it than that. (Namely the Lordship and Discipleship thing, or the process of sanctification.)

It wasn't until I was 33 that the Lordship and Discipleship thing became a real "thing" in my life.

The difficulty for us all, and it certainly was for me, is that even though I was a blood-bought son of the living God, and I had my feet firmly planted (or so I thought) in His Kingdom, I was still operating under all the rules, regulations, principles, paradigms, understanding, world view and social mores of the old system that I had been brought up to honor, ie., the system of the world. This presented a slight problem … even though I was a certified citizen of this new superior Kingdom, I could somehow neither receive nor experience the full rights and benefits of it, nor discharge the responsibilities that pertained to citizens of it because I was still firmly entrenched in the old one.

2Thessalonians 1:13b " …*God has chosen you for salvation through sanctification by the Spirit and through belief in the truth*."

So that begs the question; If you are granted permanent membership in THE club, but choose to operate under another club's rules, are you actually a real member of THE club? or are you just an "imposter" who believes that you are a member in good standing?

Unfortunately, my book didn't deal with that specific question. The book did however, do a good job at detailing the numerous "other" issues that come along with performance and perfectionism, which is essentially the stuff that we get saddled with when we enter this world and live as a part of it. It is the system of this world taught to us by none other than the evil one himself. So the system of the enemy of our souls is that which we have consciously and collectively subscribed to and are just now figuring out that we're not only not prospering under it, but we're downright miserable because of it.

The book does aptly point out who's to blame and laid out the vast majority of the problems we have agreed to take on as a result of where we now live, followed by a prayer/declaration of renouncement of all that crud.

So rather than repeat much of that work for you here I'll simply refer you to it (*The Insidious Dance*, by Jim Banks available at www.Amazon.com) for greater understanding of the multiple issues created as were growing up in an environment saturated in the ways of the world; the system created by the enemy of our souls, the devil himself.

My hope in this book is to provide you with not only a means of escape from the "Matrix," but a brief investigation of a number of Kingdom topics that are part and parcel of why our fight is so difficult. They principles are so foreign to us because of our deep indoctrination that unless Holy Spirit assists us in grabbing hold of them, we will simply reject many of them as being ill-logical and therefore of no use to us.

So my prayer is that you will read these pages with an open mind and an open heart and that they will help roll back the curtain that the enemy has pulled over your eyes so that you may see into the Kingdom more clearly.

There's more to the story ...

There was a major plot twist for this book introduced by the Lord as I was well into writing it back in early 2016. One day He said, "Stop! Stop! Stop!" I was shocked. I naturally asked, Why? He replied, *"You are making the same mistake so many have made who came before you. You are taking these principles and processing them through a mind that has been trained by the world, and altered by its wounds, and you are coming to the wrong conclusions!*" Ouch! Another trip to Africa brought home the point I had been missing all along which has changed my entire understanding, along with my Kingdom perspective. Don't know why I didn't see it. It was as plain as the nose on my face. The implications to the Kingdom were clear.

So there has been a significant reorientation in my view point which was much needed to acquire a more correct understanding of the Kingdom. That reorientation of my thinking required a major re-write of much of this material to honor it. I hope you can reap some fruit from the result of my mid-course correction.

2 Pay Close Attention

There are two principles that are pre-imminent in the Kingdom of God (or the Kingdom of Heaven), which constitutes the essence of my reorientation. Without a constant reminder of them none of us will ever really be able to grasp or understand the Kingdom itself; it's purpose, it rights and responsibilities, not to mention, its benefits, and more importantly, its' King. Neither will we be able to stay in it because the source of our motivations will always be in error. They will always have 'self' at the core somewhere, which is the antithesis of the Kingdom.

Without having these two principles firmly in place in our hearts it will largely be impossible to apply them in our lives, our daily circumstances and our relationships. These foundational elements are necessary for us to enter the Kingdom of God. Otherwise we will be trying to implement spiritual principles solely through the flesh, which never works. (Ever wonder why seemingly significant churches never seem to last? They always fall apart at some point because they fail to keep the main thing, the main thing.)

The first foundational element that must be understood is that everything about the Kingdom is ultimately about relationship, so such principles as sowing and reaping, while they are fully functional in the financial arena, they are ultimately all about relationship. The entire Bible is the story of that relationship; a love story between God and a people He chose for Himself. (John 15:16) It is about the up's and down's, the in's and out's, the highs and lows of the relationship of a faithful God with a frequently unfaithful and ungrateful people.

That's why the Lord says, "*I discipline those whom I love.*" (Rev 3:19) His ways always maximize relationship, which brings fullness of life. We have to understand the difference between discipline and punishment … and there is a vast difference. If you and cannot respond properly to the discipline of the Lord because we understand it to be an expression of His love for us then, we'll always see it as punishment. Punishment carries with it shame and sorrow and we will never be able to fully trust the one whom I believe to be the punisher. This misunderstanding is part of the reasoning of the performance orientation of the system of the world. If we do wrong then we deserve punishment, because punishment is always associated with doing evil. We certainly may not like the consequences of a mistake, but that's a far cry from intentionally doing evil, and yet that's the seriousness with which we personally view it.

Punishment also carries a measure of fear with it, so if all you can see in any correction is punishment then we become fearful of the one doing the "punishment." Being fearful of punishment begets isolation from the punisher, which is the opposite of relationship and fixes the viewpoint that rejects discipline or correction as a loving act to keep us from harm or destruction.

A child does not deserve punishment for breaking something by accident; they simply require correction (another word for discipline.) That's what loving parents do. It's all about relationship. However, when the child plays with things that can break and cause significant harm to them when it breaks, some serious training has to be accomplished for the preservation of the child. That is also a function of personal responsibility in the context of relationship.

The difficulty for many of us is that intended correction often came veiled in the anger of our parents because we disobeyed, or as a result of their fear that we'd do it again (like running out into traffic without stopping to watch for speeding vehicles) and the discipline far exceeded the infraction and therefore could only be seen as punishment for something we did wrong. If this was the way you were always disciplined then it became easier and easier for the enemy to convince you that there was either something wrong with you, or you could never do anything right. If you bought that reasoning then your only motivation for behavior modification was not to "do right," but simply to avoid punishment. Then discipline actually had the opposite effect on you.

> 1John 4:18 There is no fear in love, but perfect love casts out fear. For fear has to do with punishment, and whoever fears has not been perfected in love.
> 19 We love because he first loved us."

Unfortunately, this is the view that many have adopted because of religion. We felt like God and our fuddy-duddy authorities just wanted to stop us from having any fun and the excuse they used was whatever we wanted to do would be harmful. When our self-will (which is essentially anti-relational) fanned by immaturity is firmly in control we cast all caution to the wind and whatever feels good is right.

The second foundational element that undergirds the Kingdom is **Love**. It is such an integral part of the entire fabric of the Kingdom, that without it the Kingdom of God would become much like the kingdoms of this world; it would devolve into rules, regulations and performance. The second defining element is love because that's who created it. Love is that which drives it all, which gives it meaning and makes it effective in the lives of its adherents.

Were it not for the foundation of love none of these principles would make sense, neither could they be implemented by humans. Fortunately, the King of The Kingdom is love. He doesn't have love, He IS love, and as such His Kingdom is light-years apart from every other kingdom there is.

The obvious contrast with the Kingdom of God and the kingdom of this world is this; the Kingdom of God is founded in Love, the other is based in fear. They are polar opposites. You and I can certainly see where we have allowed fear a place in our lives, and have even re-arranged things to accommodate it; fear of man, fear of loss, fear of harm and heart ache, fear of failure, fear of the mistakes of the past invading our present and future. We are quite familiar with it because these are the underlying motivations of life taught to us by the world. It is the essence of every too the enemy has used against us to keep us from becoming who we were fully created to be, that which we struggle against daily.

When I said, "the underlying motivations of life taught to us by the world" I mean that you and I are taught to learn from our mistakes and the best way to do that is be constantly aware of what you did wrong, where you should have made a different decision, where you could have tried harder, etc. We humans are well aware of where we made a mistake or failed in some area and we are intimately aware of how each of them made us feel and what it cost us. Consequently, we learn from our mistakes. But the system of the world wants you to fear those things, not just learn from them. If you buy into it then the seeds of misery become planted and they always produce a bumper crop.

I would like to recommend a book to you that I have found to approach this subject in a way you've not seen before. Its title is *"The War of Art – Break Through The Blocks and Win Your Inner Creative Battles"* by Steven Pressfield, available on Amazon.com. It would be a quick and easy read were it not for the fact that the Lord uses it to touch all manner of insecurities, broken thought processes, self-protection mechanisms, poor habit patterns, etc., in the process.

Here is a major application of a profound principle of the Kingdom of God from 1 John 4:18-19 that would change the way we live dramatically were we able to completely lay hold of it;

"18 There is no fear in love:
but perfect love casts out fear,
because fear hath punishment; and
he that fears is not made perfect in love.
19 We love, because he first loved us." (KJV)

It is the combination of these two, love coupled with relationship, that changes every principle from a lifeless descriptor of the way things should work to a fluid, flexible, life giving format for life and blessing, the result of which is that your life can be continuously flooded with peace and joy. This is reason why Jesus came.

We have all been raised in the system of this world. We know it. We understand it and can get along well in it. It rewards us. But what happens when you try to read, absorb and adopt the principles, paradigms and world view of the Kingdom of God through a mind that is still firmly entrenched in the kingdom of this world? Everything becomes bastardized.

The conflict it creates is this; The Kingdom of Heaven is not a business, so you can't operate Kingdom enterprises (like ministries or churches) as though they were. The Kingdom of God is not a democracy. So why do we have Deacon and Elder Boards voting on every issue and running the local church as though it were a democratically operated organization? The business you are called to create or the career you are called to pursue can neither be initiated nor accomplished by committee. The Kingdom of God is founded in love, and yet we live in a world that seems to thrive on divisiveness and hatred. The Kingdom is rooted and grounded in relationship yet comparison, prejudices and competition reigns supreme.

As ugly as the above is to read, it is an apt description of what we see today all around us thriving in the country we think is the best on earth. We see one segment of politicians trying everything it can to undermine the President of the country because they believe they are smarter than, and morally superior to, the rest of the people that voted him into office. Then we see another segment of the population using violence against those they disagree with. Lawlessness abounds in a nation that is held together and prospers through rule of law.

The conflict exists for the believer because we don't really know what Kingdom principles actually are and how to walk in them apart from our understanding of how successful things operate in this world.

This is because our experience has been that the world we live in does not reward us for living life in accord with the principles of another Kingdom. We need a new viewpoint in order to start seeing things the way they are supposed to be rather than the way we have been taught that they should be.

As a believer we want our lives to count significantly for the Kingdom of God. We want our lives to have meaning and impact where it counts most - to cast a long shadow. None of us can do that without knowing what the rules of the game are. The ways of the Kingdom are not the ways of the world. There is a different set of motivators; a different set of rules and regulations; an amazingly different economy and a totally different set of values and heart. If you do not know the ways of the Kingdom of God, then you can't possibly please the King of the Kingdom.

3   The Foundation

My wife (Patricia) and I have been in the inner healing and deliverance biz for nigh unto 40 years now. The last 15 of which have been full time. We have seen a lot of strange stuff over those years and have been continually amazed at how ignorant the vast majority of Christians are about the Kingdom of God, despite the fact that it is specifically mentioned 70 times in the Bible; 69 of them in the New Testament (KJV). The phrase, Kingdom of Heaven, is mentioned 33 times in the New Testament and both are coupled with some very some very important declarations and commandments with a promise.

My viewpoint is that if you continue to apply the world's recommended solutions to your difficult personal problems, you may still be trying to solve them on your death bed.

Now the most common difficulties that many of my clients report tends to fall into the same category, but is experienced (or at least realized) from several different perspectives is this;

1) I've lost who I am over the years (assuming they ever really knew that person),

2) My heart feels dead, I have no up or downs and my relationships are fed up with it,

3) I'm stuck/lost/frozen and don't know where to go or what to do next, and the ubiquitous,

4) I no longer have a relationship with God and can't seem to find Him anywhere. He moved and left no forwarding address – and I'm stuck here with all these knuckleheads and I can't take it anymore!

Many regularly point to the weight of life-long symptoms of depression and anxiety, panic attacks, the results of PTSD, great betrayals, abuse, and disappointment in their lives, rejection and abandonment, potentially coupled with long term physical issues that have become debilitating and have sapped all hope of recovery and a 'normal' life. To make matters worse, these maladies have robbed them of the ability to make a good living, so they've not sought competent and consistent help to resolve the issues. They have stood in prayer lines, made appointments for prayer and personal ministry on numerous occasions, but have never committed themselves to comprehensive long-term therapies … or a discipleship relationship.

What I am proposing for most folks in this situation is 1) go to someone and deal with the spiritual implications of your difficulty, then 2) connect on a long term basis with a healer/mentor to deal with the root belief systems you have created that keep you stuck in the mess. That latter process can be crudely described as "get your butt out of the Matrix, then get your head and your heart into the Kingdom."

The reason behind all these maladies is very simple – it's fear. Fear is at the heart of the system of this world. When we are very young (5 or 6 and under) we simply want to be loved by our parents. That means being noticed, being appreciated, people being excited to be with us. When that doesn't happen because our parents work two jobs, they are self absorbed, unavailable emotionally, addicted or worse yet, abusive, we will work extra hard to get the kind of attention we feel we need and deserve. If that works we try harder to make it happen again for us – then we're hooked. If our efforts don't produce results, we still try hard because the way this works is this; to fail means there's something wrong with me. I cannot possibly let that happen and I will work like hell to keep anything or anybody from saying it, including myself. Fear is at the root of it all.

The problem is that we are actually ratifying our worst fears by our actions to defend against it. Most of it becomes a desperate effort to create personal value for ourselves by establishing a persona that we think is more likeable/lovable/less rejectable – one that is really unlike ourselves, because that one is flawed somehow. In the process we can no longer live out of the heart we were created with, we have to process all of life through our head, assessing every person, activity and event for its potential to hurt us, wound us and prove that we have no value. That takes an incredible amount of emotional energy to do over an extended period of time. By the time a typical individual reaches 30 years of age they have begun to run out of energy to be continually vigilant to recognize all harmful agents and the heartaches of a lifetime are knocking at their door saying it needs their company. When they have fought it off as long as they can, that's when they come to me searching for an answer.

(Interestingly, if your parents were also perfectionists it's tough to make to it 30 without cratering. If you are extremely intelligent it is possible to make it to 40, but the crash landing is brutal and a few have even been fatal.) I am thoroughly convinced that this crash is what's being described as "a mid-life crisis." People find that their values have to change or they'll go crazy, or worse.

So the transition out of the system of the world into the Kingdom requires all manner of changes to the way you have lived, processed life, your world view, your relationships and responsibilities, not to mention, the way you think. Facing the fear of a change is the toughest part of it of it all because success is still the name of the world's game. It has been made worse by the American bastardization of the gospel, which says,

"If I do right, everything will be right."

We can point to numerous scriptures that seem to verify the truth of that statement and they seem to almost say the exact same thing. However, this is one of the tricks of the enemy. The scriptures actually says, *"do as I say and I (God) will give you peace, even in the face of your enemy's (the devil) attempts to kill you."* Jesus reframed it by saying in John 16:33, *"In the world you will have tribulation ... but fear not ..."* inferring that in this world you have a sworn enemy who will do anything within his power to fulfill the purposes that Jesus declared he was here for, (John 10:10) *"steal, kill and destroy."* The implication is that even if you do right, everything may not work out all right because you have an enemy who is continually at work trying to throw a monkey wrench into the works.

Further, you can eat right, exercise, watch your weight and your cholesterol and still die of some dread disease because we live in a fallen world full of folks who make bad decisions for the sake of convenience, money, power or fame, or even out of ignorance, creating a myriad of pits for us to fall into. For generations they have polluted our environment, put all manner of drugs and chemicals into our food and water, and polluted our air, making it a very hazardous place for you and me – even if you do everything right.

The thought behind *"If I do right, everything will be right"* is actually fear of failure. If I do right and it doesn't work out right, then it's not my fault and nobody can blame me. Another variation on this theme is related to games. Many folks who struggle in this area can be heard thinking, *"If you'll just tell me the rules, I'll play."* The reasoning is that the rules keep me safe and in knowing the rules I can make an accurate assessment of the risks of failure. Playing the game without knowing what the rules are insures failure. That can't happen. It cannot be my fault.

I follow a fellow by the name of Arthur Burk, (www.theslg.com) whom the Lord was poking on earlier in this past year (2016) regarding the topic of fear. Arthur summarized his personal prayer inquiry as follows, "*Where have I re-ordered my life to accommodate fear?*"

If we are the least bit honest with ourselves, the answer(s) to that question can be quite long. As I none-too-gracefully age, there are a number of unanswered questions posed that are basically a response to fear;

a) I suffered through a bout with colon cancer six years ago. My father died of bone cancer 7 years after its first appearance as prostate cancer. My brother was diagnosed with prostate cancer 12 years ago and is now suffering with brain cancer. So future health and longevity is an issue. How do I provide for my wife in the event of a shorter life span?

b) We are in fulltime ministry and we live financially by faith. Much of our income is a function of ministering in one-on-one sessions. As we begin doing pastoral care for long-term missionaries overseas, who are caring for orphans, we have no time to do one-on-one sessions anymore. What will those changes require of us financially?

c) What happens if there is significant inflation or we have another economic disaster?

d) In the USA, ObamaCare has created a major healthcare mess. The average healthcare premium for a family in 2017 is $18,000. The number of younger participants is now less than half of original their projections, forcing higher premiums for everyone else. Even the subsidized plans are too expensive for many. Congress reneged on funding the subsidies and pulled 50% of the funding. Fines for not having health insurance have increased to $1,250.00 (2016). What is the health insurance climate going to look like for us going forward?

e) Then there's the issue with our kids. Our oldest son joined the Army as a Medic, which if the state of the world remains as is that means he's probably gonna do a tour or two in Iraq or Afghanistan. Not exactly what former military men want to see for their kids.

f) The agenda of liberals in America has purposely painted Christians as angry judgmental bedfellows of the Westboro Baptist Church whackjobs. When coupled with the government's desire to provide peace and safety to every citizen, What does that portend for our future as ministers in or outside of the organized church?

g) As the political tension grows between liberals and conservatives and our society leans more and more toward socialist policies increasing taxation is inevitable, severely pressing those on fixed incomes.

h) And there's probably a dozen other things that have some level of concern connected to them that I don't even recognize as yet.

Well, it's as obvious as the nose on my face, I have to continue to trust God as I have in the past. But fear consistently knocks at the door in an attempt to bring into question every place where even a shred of doubt still lingers. So if there is any place where the precepts of performance still holds sway, the habits that we began to build decades ago (based in fear) come into play once again ... which lead us to do something to re-arrange our lives to accommodate fear once again.

The system is relentless. Performance and perfectionism requires us to live by the rules, even if they are of our own making. We live our lives amassing a set of them that dictates to us how to avoid failure, achieve success and how to manage the risks inherent in all activity. Since they are so good for us we naturally assume that they are certainly good for everyone else as well. So we judge others by their ability to keep our rules, even if they have no idea that they exist.

Scripture warns us not to judge because we'll soon be judged for the very thing we judge others for. (Matthew 7:1, Luke 6:37, Romans 2:1) What goes around comes around. Yet the rules we created demand that they be kept, so we judge and in defense chose to call it discernment; the unintended consequence of fear.

The ultimate problem we have is the battle between two worlds, two systems, flesh and spirit. The Apostle Paul writes to us in his letter to the Romans, Chapter 12,

*"**1** I beseech you therefore, brethren, by the mercies of God, that ye present your bodies a living sacrifice, holy, acceptable unto God, which is your reasonable service.*
*2 And **be not conformed to this world: but be transformed** by the renewing of your mind, that you may prove what is that good, and acceptable, and perfect, will of God."*

My view is that in order for us to enter the Kingdom of God in fullness we are going to have to rid ourselves of the blinders (the un-renewed mind) that have required us to call the rules and principles of this world the highest good; those that have continued to blind us to the truth and freedom offered by pursuing and devoting ourselves to the Kingdom of God and its King.

Jesus died, was buried and resurrected, and now sits at the right hand of The Father so that we can have all the benefits of the Kingdom and the power to do all that is asked of us. But just like salvation, we have to make a choice to receive it. We have to make a choice to enter the fullness of the Kingdom, which means we have to choose to bail out of the one we are in and renounce all its rules and regulations that have governed our lives since we came into this world, so that we are free to choose the principles of the Kingdom of God and live in obedience to its King.

You can start that process by praying the following prayer I have provided next. I have replicated the prayer noted in *The Insidious Dance* book here for you to recite because you can't easily enter into the Kingdom of God in fullness unless you have broken all the agreements with the old system that you are still adhering to.

"Father, in the name of Your son Jesus Christ, I ask Your forgiveness for coming into agreement with the system of this world, the teachings of the enemy himself, and for adopting his values and his system of weights and measures. I repent for making myself the god of my own world and believing that I could control my circumstances and dictate my own outcomes. Forgive me!

In the mighty name of Jesus, on behalf of myself and my entire blood line, I break, shatter, cut off, and destroy all agreement with perfectionism and the system of this world, including the one who taught it to us all. On behalf of myself and my family line, I renounce its teachings, its principles, its rules and regulations, and any of its authority in my life and those of my family members. I ask Father, that you forgive me for not only agreeing with this system but teaching its principles to others as though they were pre-emanate for all creation. I was wrong! I ask You, Father, to break any and all curses from me and from my generational line that were established because of our agreement and participation with this iniquitous system.

I ask You, Father, to disconnect me and my family line from any demonic entities that have been assigned to us as a result of our repeated agreement with the system of the enemy.

Will You also cancel any demonic strategies that have been planned against us to hold us, and its principles, in this place? Would You also please re-assign every Godly entity to me and my family line that is necessary for each of us to fulfill our purposes here on earth?

As an act of my will, I renounce and lay down all the rules and regulations that I have amassed over the years that have determined how to achieve success, avoid failure, and manage the risk of potential failure. I choose to no longer live by slavery to the law and its curses, even if it is ones I created. In Jesus' name, by the power of the Holy Spirit, I choose to now live by the law of life in Christ Jesus. I ask that You show me every habit pattern that I have created that is built upon the performance/perfectionist system I just resigned from and grant me the grace to establish new habit patterns that are Kingdom oriented.

I ask you to show me every belief system, every paradigm of thought, every portion of my world view that agrees with the system of the enemy. I choose to open my eyes to what you show me and I ask that you grant me insight into every principle that I have adopted. I ask that you grant me the grace to make different decisions, all of which agree with the precepts of your Word.

I ask your forgiveness where I have been so bold as to establish my own values, my own sense of worth, my own understanding of "right and wrong" that accommodated my flesh and my self-will. I willfully declare that you are right and I am wrong. Teach me your ways.

Henceforth, I choose to grant myself the grace to fail, to not get it right, to make mistakes. I loose myself from fear of failure and renounce any allegiance I had to that spirit and its rule over me. I take that ground back and I give to the Lord Jesus Christ for Him to rule and reign over.

I break, shatter, cut off, and destroy all allegiance to a critical sprit. I command you to go from me now. I ask, Father, that You restore to me the Spirit of Joy that I gave up when I embraced this ungodly system. I ask that You restore my sense of humor, and the ability to laugh at my own mistakes, and to not take myself so seriously. Teach me how to play again.

I choose to live free of self-condemnation and self-imposed guilt and shame. I will no longer accuse and abuse myself by continually rehearsing where I blew it, where I could have done better, or where I made a mistake. As your Word declares to me, "Life and death are in the power of the tongue" (Proverbs 18:21). I will henceforth guard my mouth so that I continually speak only life (see Deuteronomy 30:19) over myself and my affairs. I also choose to stop judging others by that same set of rules and regulations that I set up for myself, and I give them the same permission to fail and not it right that I extend to myself and my family members.

I break, shatter, cut off, and destroy all allegiance to a spirit of self-hate. I command you to go from me now. I repent for agreeing with the enemy that I was not worthy, not valuable, not loveable, even for thinking or saying that there was something wrong with me. I choose to agree with You, Father, that what You made was good. Forgive me for thinking otherwise. I also choose to believe what You say about me, above what I have been taught or learned while under that system.

I choose to forgive my father and mother, and any other authority figure in my life, for disappointing me, for not treating me as I thought they should, even for abusing and mistreating me. I forgive them for not accepting me as the gift

I was to them; for not accepting me as I was, for using me as though I was property to do with as they pleased. I ask You, Father, to forgive them as well. I repent for any judgments that I made against them and cancel any vows that I made that said I would not be like them in any way, nor model their behavior. I ask Your forgiveness for dishonoring them.

I ask Your forgiveness for shutting down my heart and believing that I could defend myself from experiencing more pain and heart ache on my own terms. Forgive me for taking matters into my own hands rather than depending upon the power of Your Spirit to heal and nurture me. I choose to once again open my heart to live rather than try to figure everything out on my own.

Father, where I have shut down my ear to You and damaged my ability to walk in all You created me for by dependence upon myself, I repent and ask You to restore me to full functionality once again. I ask You to restore any damage done to any portion of my body while I was under the spell cast by this system. I ask You to once again draw the line between my natural mind and its instincts of self preservation and my spirit, so that I may quickly discern the difference between what is Your way and those of my own devices.

I ask You, Father, to restore to me the blessings of my family line that I and my family have forgone as a result of participating with this system. If there are any purposes that You had in Your heart for me and my family line to achieve that were thwarted by our allegiance to the system of the world, I ask that You renew them, call them forward, and I ask that You grant us the grace and impart whatever gifting, skill or anointing that is necessary to complete them, that nothing You have desired would remain unaccomplished by me or my family line.

Finally Father, I ask that You teach me how to love with my whole heart, not just giving portions of myself as a means of getting what I need at the moment. Reorient my thoughts so that I am able to love first rather than counting the cost and trying to determine if it's worth it. I choose to love and to be known for it.

Father, I thank You for hearing my prayer."

What I urge you to do is pray this prayer at least once a week for a month and see the difference that it makes in how you encounter and perceive events in your life. I have been doing this with clients for the better part of a year now, probably once a week or so, and it has made an enormous difference because we collectively don't have any idea how engrained we are in the system of this world. It has been taught and modeled to us by every institution we have been a part of; family, schools, jobs, military, government, the political system, sports teams, clubs and societies, there is nothing left untouched by it, including family, marriage, business and social relationships. It's time we entered the real Kingdom, not the one we are promised if we do well.

4   As You Dig IN ...

What follows is a series of topics on some of the principles of the Kingdom of God that we not only need to understand, but we have to allow to change our viewpoint and the resulting habit patterns that we have adopted. Also, you need to understand that this is not by any means an exhaustive list of them.

Don't blast through this book going from topic to topic without spending some time with the Lord asking Him, "Where have I resisted this idea? Where have I intentionally chosen to adopt and maintain the principles taught to me by the system of this world? And how has it impacted my life? Where have I chosen not to love and to hold as sacred the relationships you have given me?

Here is an interaction with the Lord I had several months ago that may help give you some additional impetus to fully process what I am attempting to convey ...

(Jim) "Lord I am grateful for the year we've had – for your great faithfulness, your forgiveness and mercy – your revelation and anointing and for your opportunities."

(God) *"Those are like a song to me. They gladden my heart and cause my face to turn to you.*

You live in an ungrateful nation, among an ungrateful people; those who believe that everything they have received and possess has been because of their cunning ways and the power of their own hand, or is the product of their own creative mind. They do not even choose to consider that there may be a more powerful beneficent force at work. Much of what they have is because of the prayers and deeds of the righteous; and they abhor them; fight against them and the very thing that has brought the blessings they strive so hard to hold on to.

... Come out from them. Do not entangle yourself in the affairs of the nation. Do not let it take you down with it.

Am I going to punish the righteous with the evil? No, but I am judging the world within them. Come out from among them that you be not judged as well. You are going to see evil on a scale you have never witnessed before - and all in the name of peace and progress ... and you will see it with significant local manifestations. Your own city is not immune.

Understand, that I have promised those in the kingdom food/drink/clothing/shelter. (Matthew 6). *When you try to hang on to more than that, evil is birthed."*

      The Apostle Paul made this statement; that we are in the world, not of it. He said it for much the same reason that I wrote this book.

      This last election cycle (2016) culminated in a victory for Republicans that many liberal Democrats have not only struggled with, but for more than a few has brought a real personal crisis. We had a couple of young men in our church who completely lost their way as a result. One of them stated, "I don't even believe in God anymore." I am not sure that this was simply an expression of the emotion connected to unrealized expectations, but it illuminates the absolute fragility of a life anchored in something other than the King and His Kingdom. It is a perfect example of the futility in anchoring your hope in something solely of this world. Gross disappointment is its only reward. If our hope is in anything other than God and His ability to take care of us, we are in for a very rough ride, and the enemy will make sure of that!

Since that election we have found another interesting phenomenon arise; that of willfully working to thwart the activities of the sitting Administration, whether you are in or outside of it. This is obviously more akin to strategies of third world politics than what we are accustomed to in the US. The difficulty with this is multifold but simply put the division it sows insures that the Republic is on its last legs and chaos is just around the corner, which will invite a "benevolent dictator" to step up – end of the Republic and democracy as well.

These are very difficult times, in which each of us needs to know which Kingdom we are going to follow. The Kingdom you chose is the Kingdom that comes. The Kingdom of this world comes at a very painful price, now and in the age to come.

5 A Kingdom Perspective

The problem we Christians have had in grasping the Kingdom is that we are looking at matters that are strictly spiritual through an earthly eye and interpreting it through minds that have been trained by the world. In so doing we have elevated the wrong characteristics of the Kingdom far above the actual core values of the Kingdom. We have mistakenly thought that many of the elements that bring success in the world are actually Kingdom principles that have infiltrated the world. For instance, I have taught on 2 Corinthians 5:20a *"Now then we are Ambassadors for Christ ..."* Webster's 1833 Dictionary defines it as; *"A minister of the highest rank employed by one prince or state, at the court of another, to manage the public concerns of his own prince or state, and representing the power and dignity of his sovereign. They are also called ministers."*

In truth, we are ambassadors, ministers and representatives of a superior Kingdom sent to a foreign one (in which we physically reside) to demonstrate the superiority of that heavenly Kingdom in comparison to the rules, regulations, laws, and principles of this earthly kingdom and those that rule over it. Since our citizenship is elsewhere, we choose only to follow the laws of this realm as dictated by the laws of our own, choosing to practically demonstrate to the citizens of this realm the ascendant supremacy of our own, and the dominance of its benevolent sovereign head.

The primary means by which we Christians have historically chosen to express our demonstrations of the Kingdom is actually a limitation of it; prophetic words, Words of Knowledge, healings and deliverances, etc; in essence, exclusively exercising the power gifts. These were certainly things demonstrated repeatedly during the ministry of Christ here on earth, but were by no means the limit of it, and "It is enough for the disciple that he be as his master, and the servant as his lord." (Matt 10:25) Jesus spent 3 ½ years in the company of His disciples (learners), teaching them on a daily basis not only what the Kingdom was, but what it meant, and demonstrating it every day through his speech and actions. This was a personal demonstration of His commands to us personally recorded in Matthew 28:19-20; disciple the nations.

The idea behind limiting our expressions of the Kingdom to the operation of the power gifts falls in line with the teachings of the system of this world; **might makes right**. If I kick out a demon, then say I love you, does that mean I've met the qualifications for Kingdom citizenship or relationship? I think not.

In fact, Jesus even said as much,

> *Matthew 7:19-23 " Every tree that bringeth not forth good fruit is hewn down, and cast into the fire.*
> *20 Wherefore by their fruits ye shall know them.*
> *21 Not every one that saith unto me, Lord, Lord, shall enter into the kingdom of heaven; but he that doeth the will of my Father which is in heaven.*
> *22 Many will say to me in that day, Lord, Lord, have we not prophesied in thy name? and in thy name have cast out devils? and in thy name done many wonderful works?*
> *23 And then will I profess unto them, **I never knew you: depart from me**, ye that work iniquity." (KJV)*

For those of you who have majored exclusively on the power gifts, this is not good news. The good fruit that he was talking about in this passage (v.19) was not prophetic words, healings, Words of Knowledge or Wisdom, or deliverance, but doing good deeds and giving good gifts to your neighbor, taking care of the poor, the widows and the orphans. Not power, but love and intentionally sowing into relationships. How many powerful ministers have you known who were unbearable tyrants in their home, as well as relational jackasses in the conduct of ministry business?

So what non-power oriented demonstrations of the Kingdom do we need to consider.

Well, first of all, let's back away a bit and get a larger view of the landscape. The entire Bible is a book solely about a relationship; a relationship that God chose to have with a special group of people. It is about the ups and downs, and the ins and outs of that relationship.

The New Testament is the part where we non-Jews are included in that relationship. It is the declaration of God's love for us saying that even while we were still His enemy, He loved us and still chose us. This is a direct expression of His character. So there is the requirement that to be in the Kingdom, we have to have a relationship with Him. In fact, we have to be one with Him. (John 17) He so wanted to be with us that when we finally chose Him (salvation), He sent His Holy Spirit to join with ours on an individual basis.

In John 15:14-15, we find that there is also a depth of relationship that the Lord desires wherein we move from a convert, to a disciple, then onto friendship. This level of relationship implies that we, like Jesus, are continually doing the will of our heavenly Father because, like Jesus, we are doing what we see Him doing and only saying what we hear Him saying. (Matthew 7:21, John 5:30 and 15:19)

The relationship with Him should propel us to want to walk in all the power gifts, but the motivation has to be from a heart of love and relationship, not one of doing work, or proving a point. Our performance should come from a loving desire to please the King, not from a place that desires for the King to be happy with me because I'm doing big important stuff for Him. We should not work for God, but instead with Him.

The requirement for Kingdom relationship doesn't stop there. It is expected that it will be extended to others who believe in the King as well, and then, like Him, extended to those who are yet His enemies. When you take stock of the status of the American church today, as well as our individual belief systems, we see that relationship with our fellow believers (joint heirs) fails to meet the King's expectation of the citizens of the Kingdom. In fact, for many it seems to have become their duty, even their identity, to point out their particular differences from the other factions, as though it confirmed their holiness to the Lord.

In central Kentucky, there is a group that identifies themselves as "Separate Baptists." I'm not sure what that means other than by the admission of one of their own adherents when asked what the difference was, "Well, I'm not sure. We're just not like the rest of them Baptists." Well, I'm so happy for you all, but if "Judge Not" is one of the basic tenets of citizenship in the Kingdom, and you are also required to "forgive" and to "Love" those who are not like you, including your enemies (Matthew 5:44), then there is an undeniable question regarding the legitimacy of your claim to Kingdom citizenship.

This is not rocket science here folks. Jesus meant what He said and said what He meant. Love, forgive, don't judge and walk in the closest level of relationship that is possible for you. Anything else, for any other reason, is NOT of the King, or the Kingdom of God.

Philippians 2:1-4 *"So if there is any encouragement in Christ, any comfort from love, any participation in the Spirit, any affection and sympathy, 2 complete my joy by being of the same mind, having the same love, being in full accord and of one mind. 3 Do nothing from rivalry or conceit, but in humility count others more significant than yourselves. 4 Let each of you look not only to his own interests, but also to the interests of others."* (ESV)

Now I understand that there are differences in worship, preaching and teaching styles among our various denominations and sects, even slight differences in beliefs. Some of which we are more comfortable with than others and we naturally gravitate to the ones we are most at ease with. However, in so doing, we also separate ourselves along the lines of comparable values, similar lifestyles, education, and race – not to mention the sect we were raised in or around. The problem with this is that as long as we doggedly hold on to our preferences, shunning others in the process, we cannot readily claim Kingdom citizenship any more than those who identify themselves as "Separate What-evers" because of their judgments and exclusivity.

We have so clung to the minutia of doctrinal differences and how we practice them that we have utterly failed to consider the foundational requirement of the Kingdom of God; authentic relationship with Him and His other subjects, thereby ensuring that we are not actually Kingdom citizens at all, but Christianized impostors. The principle behind the elevation of distinctions that separates us has been taught to us by the world; **If I am right in what I believe, then you are wrong**. (Solely because it is different.)

As Christians, of whatever denomination, we are no doubt aware of this verse;

John 13:34 *"A new commandment I give unto you, That ye love one another; as I have loved you."*

So what particular element of your current theology, denominational pride and prejudices, or belief system is preventing you from obeying this command? If John 13:34 doesn't do it for you take a gander at this;

1John_4:7-12 *" Beloved, let us love one another: for love is of God; and every one that loveth is born of God, and knoweth God.*

*8 **He that loveth not knoweth not God**; for God is love.*

9 In this was manifested the love of God toward us, because that God sent his only begotten Son into the world, that we might live through him. 10 Herein is love, not that we loved God, but that he loved us, and sent his Son to be the propitiation for our sins.

11 Beloved, if God so loved us, we ought also to love one another.

12 No man hath seen God at any time. If we love one another, God dwelleth in us, and his love is perfected in us.

*1John_4:20 -21 **"If a man say, I love God, and hateth his brother, he is a liar: for he that loveth not his brother whom he hath seen, how can he love God whom he hath not seen?***

21 And this commandment have we from him, That he who loveth God love his brother also. (KJV)

The case for the requirement to love is therein is pretty bluntly stated and its conclusion needs no interpretation.

Are you aware that the number one reason why long-term missionaries leave the field? It is because of major relational issues with other long-term missionaries. If missionaries cannot love one another then what are they actually doing?

There are also numerous ministries and fellowships (I hesitate to call them churches) that feel it their God-given duty to "protect" you from the deceivers and imposters and have therefore judged almost everyone as such because they are not exactly like them. Folks, this isn't discernment, this is blatant arrogance that your knowledge and understanding is greater than anyone;

Luke 9:50 *"And Jesus said unto him, Forbid him not: for he that is not against us is for us."* Later He said,

John10:27-29 "My sheep hear my voice, and I know them, and they follow me:
28 And I give unto them eternal life; and they shall never perish, neither shall any man pluck them out of my hand.
29 My Father, which gave them me, is greater than all; and no man is able to pluck them out of my Father's hand."

This kind of thing grieves me greatly because when unbelievers witness this sort of thing they become as judgmental as those who spout it and decide that all Christians are as harsh and judgmental as these folks. If you are supporting such people financially, including your own church, or if the shoe fits personally, stop it immediately and sow into ministries that are actually being a blessing, rather than throwing dust in the air.

Charles Wesley (Methodist) and George Whitefield (an Anglican Calvinist) were very different theologically. Charles Wesley wrote a letter to Whitefield towards the end of both their lives. He said something to this effect; *"We loved more when we knew less."*

We were created for relationship. Relationship is the essence of the Kingdom. It is the only thing that brings us true fulfillment and continual life. It is the lifeblood of community – and the Kingdom. It is the process of knowing and being known (Matt 7:21-23) in spite of our differences, or perhaps because of our differences, for it is actually our differences that make us valuable to one another.

We tend to approach knowing and being known with some trepidation because we don't want folks (much less God) to know "everything" about us, for they might reject us, or use what they know against us. So the fight for relational connection with your fellow man becomes a delicate fitful dance; too far, not near enough, How much can I say and still look good? How much pain can I expose without disclosing my need? How much is too much information and not really expressive of how I feel? I want to feel good about saying it, but not simultaneously reveal my weakness. And yet, if I am not "known" I will never feel connected.

 There are always risks inherent in relationship and community. As citizens of the Kingdom, we must face them in ourselves and in others with love, patience, and bravery. We must not be afraid to encounter and completely resolve the hidden motivations of our heart, along with the anti-Kingdom principles taught to us by living in the world, and particularly the ones that we have transported into our expressions of life in the Kingdom, for they are the very things that will keep us from experiencing life to the fullest and will eventually keep us out of the Kingdom.

> *Matthew 8:11-12 "And I say unto you, That many shall come from the east and west, and shall sit down with Abraham, and Isaac, and Jacob, in the kingdom of heaven. 12 But the children of the kingdom shall be cast out into outer darkness: there shall be weeping and gnashing of teeth." (KJV)*

This verse is interesting because it emphatically states that everyone must have their own relationship with the King. One cannot be a Kingdom citizen based solely on the citizenship of their parents or the heritage of a lengthy Christian lineage. One cannot enter the club as a guest. Hanging around those who are in the club is an insufficient qualification for membership in the club.

Now speaking of "hanging around club (Kingdom) members" brings up another subject that needs some air time; discipleship.

> Matthew 28: 18-20 *"And Jesus came and said to them, "All authority in heaven and on earth has been given to me. 19 Go therefore and **make disciples of all nations**, baptizing them in the name of the Father and of the Son and of the Holy Spirit, 20 **teaching them to observe all that I have commanded you**. And behold, I am with you always, to the end of the age."* (ESV)

My wife and I are acquainted with several large ministries who are doing some amazing things all over the world. But we have found that each of them has a major unresolved issue. They tend to focus exclusively on evangelism and do so little discipleship that those efforts are virtually meaningless in comparison. I feel that as a result of their singular focus that they are actually failing to fulfill the command of Jesus to disciple the nations.

In order to disciple a nation, you have to meaningfully impact every aspect of the nation's culture for the Kingdom. This means making a decided impact on the government, the education system, the military, healthcare, religion (the church), media, commerce, the family and so on. But if your efforts begin and end with evangelism, and maybe starting a series of churches, all you have touched is one small segment of the culture that will in time, be overwhelmed by the others, which will naturally be in opposition to it, or worse, the message of that evangelized group will be a sorry mixture of the gospel and local beliefs.

You have to admit that Jesus is a pretty smart guy and that He knows how to capture entire people groups (nations) for His father's Kingdom. Why should we limit what He had in mind by focusing only on one aspect of discipling?

I am in no way discounting the importance of evangelism, but if all it results in is recruiting members to the club and does not impact every element of their culture, then there is serious reason to question whether you are actually fulfilling the commands of Christ.

I have no doubt that Christ in someone has the ability to change the culture of an individual, but if you have ever been to Africa and witnessed the lack of integrity in second and third generation believers because the church did nothing to impact the balance of the culture, then you have to conclude that Jesus really knew why He was telling us to do what He told us to do

We must help raise up those who have been called to important platforms in business, in politics, in healthcare, in media, etc., for evangelism and discipleship must make its way into every aspect of the marketplace where the vast majority of people live much of their lives. I will pray for a couple of dozen soldiers over the course of a year, but a man or woman in uniform has the ability to impact dozens of them every day; people you or I will never be able to touch.

Some of you will say that the church is made up of people from all walks of life who can share their faith with others in their field of endeavor. That's true, but if you are not discipling them, all you get is a convert who cannot replicate himself. An African pastor who travels often to the states said recently, "The church has millions of Christians, but only 0.3% of them are believers."

The Kingdom requires more of us than to only know that God exists because of a salvation experience. It requires discipleship for us and through us. "*If you love me, you will keep my commandments.*"

6 Kingdom Government

Among the first things to know about the Kingdom of God is that   it is not a democracy. First of all, it is **HIS Kingdom**, not that our King is against democracy or any other form of government, but that just isn't how His Kingdom works. Secondly, The King is the sole determiner of what happens in His Kingdom. It's not that He doesn't want your input, but when the King is omniscient, all-knowing, all-seeing, omnipresent and all powerful, He simply has no need for advisors or counselors. When you see the end from the beginning, you have absolutely no use for a life coach or a sports psychologist to help you stay on your game.

He can comfortably let you plan your way, but he orders your steps so that that which He has planned for your life, and the lives of others, can actually come to fruition so that nothing is left to chance … all because of His love for you. He is effectively in control, and yet you still have free will. If you chose to destroy your relationships (and your life) you have all the freedom you need to accomplish it. He will put roadblocks in your way to get you to change your mind, but in the end, you can do as you wish.

If a small child runs out into a busy major thoroughfare, a loving parent runs and snatches the child out of the danger, swats them on the butt and attempts to inform them of the danger and warns them to never do that again … all because of love. The child is totally unaware that death or dismemberment could be the result of their venture. They have to be taught what is dangerous and what is safe.

So it is with God. His love for you compels Him to occasionally discipline you so that you may avoid future danger and possible destruction. When we are young we interpret these strictures as rules that are meant to deprive us of fun and excitement. We are generally ignorant of the consequences of sin and our lack of discernment. When we are older, we have a totally different viewpoint because we've had some life experiences to teach us about the wide range of personal destruction available to us as a result of specific behaviors and actions.

This is the marvelous thing about our creator and King. He understands the ramifications and knows the fullness of the effect of every decision we make, whether it is for our good, or for our harm. It is His desire to grow us into His likeness so that we, in turn, can inform others of what we have learned and can be witnesses to the blessing of listening and obeying the King.

I wish that I could say that I have consistently walked the life of faith. But I would be lying. In my younger years, I was as self-willed as anyone on the planet and I was hell-bent on living my life as I wanted. That didn't turn out too well. There are still occasions when the Lord has to put my motivation in check. I have learned the hard way that living in the Kingdom is a whole lot more blessed than trying to live outside of it. The King knows what works and what doesn't and it is His desire that your life is marked by peace and joy. The King not only knows what works and what doesn't, but what the consequence of a series of poor decisions today will produce for you 20 or 30 years down the road. A sure future and a firm hope are only available as we are one with the King.

> Psalms 103:19 "The LORD has prepared his throne in the heavens; and his kingdom rules over all."

Deuteronomy 10:14 "Behold, the heaven and the heaven of heavens is the LORD'S thy God, the earth also, with all that therein is."

Psalms 135:6 "Whatsoever the LORD pleased, that did he in heaven, and in earth, in the seas, and all deep places." (KJV)

Let me give you another example of the sovereign nature of the King of The Kingdom. The Word says,

Romans 11:29 "For the gifts and calling of God are without repentance."

How many complete jackasses have you met that are uncannily proficient in giving prophetic words, successful at praying for physical and emotional healing, etc.? We are often prone to wonder if God knew what He was doing at the time He gave that gift to that person. In the last 16 years, I have had the fortune (good and bad) to be around a number of high-profile ministers in the body of Christ and a large number of them have turned out to be self-absorbed, ill-mannered, socially incompetent jerk. Are they anointed? Yes, darn it. Are they doing great things for God in these meetings? Yes, God is certainly moving, but He also moves in the lives of people following fires, hurricanes and earthquakes.

By the foregoing, it is probably obvious that I hold those folk in something less than high esteem, and you would be right. I have real difficulty in wanting to be around people who are so difficult socially. I pray God did not make them that way, but the characteristic is so common that it is either the case, or the stresses of that calling and gifting drive them there. Folks, you cannot choose to be anointed. That's God's decision. But maturity is another matter and those who choose not mature in love and relationship will find themselves walking alone well before their time is done.

Because I am a supposed to be a Kingdom dweller, my response to them should be a lot more loving and kind because that's the way it's going to be, whether I like it or not. (According to my memory there's only a couple of instances in scripture where God changed His mind. That covers a minimum of 7,000 years.) God isn't about to change them or remove them from their calling, or strip them of their gifting and anointing because they are not warm and fuzzy individuals. Apparently, He has a plan and a purpose that I'm not aware of and I just need to agree with Him that they are doing their part to the best of their ability.

> 2 Timothy 2:20 *"But in a great house there are not only vessels of gold and of silver, but also of wood and of earth; and some to honor, and some to dishonor." (KJV)*

And in the process, I cannot badmouth them for what they are doing, even if I think it is harmful to them and others. I have to willfully choose to forgive and honor people with my words, even as the Lord does as they are leaving a trail of wounded people in their wake.

Love forgives. Love honors. Love chooses to think the best and speak the best. Love does not keep a record of wrongs. Love is neither prideful nor spiteful. Love hopes for the best in all things and believes for good in all things. (1 Corinthians 13)

7 Anticipation

Here's a big clue for believers – you can't see the Kingdom unless you are looking for it. Kingdom anticipation; the fruit of it is demonstrated by God Himself on your behalf and most likely through others in response to its appearance in you. In many cases, it may begin with the experience of noticing a change in your viewpoint and your own attitudes.

> Luke 17:20-21 *"Being asked by the Pharisees when the kingdom of God would come, he answered them, "The kingdom of God is not coming with signs to be observed, 21 nor will they say, 'Look, here it is!' or 'There!' for behold, the **kingdom of God is in the within you**."*

Often you cannot see what you are not looking for, and you certainly cannot see it when your eyes are closed to what you need to see. If you are not looking for it (anticipating the favor supplied by God) you will never recognize it when it appears. You'll ascribe it to something else entirely.

It happens to us all the time. One of the favorite things the Lord loves to do for His people is to show them favor. For instance; several months ago I signed up online for a department store's discount club. I have been getting their discount codes on sale merchandise for months and had never used any of them. Since we were going back to Africa in a couple of months I was much more aware of what sort of wardrobe was needed.

I wandered into this department store and looked at the merchandise that was on clearance. Ah ha! The tag had 50% off the previously listed price. I found two shirts and took them to the register. The Spirit then prompted me to look at my phone where this store's discount texts come in. Another 50% off!! Then the lady at the register asked if I was a member of their Tuesday Shopper's Club – the membership number was also in the text – Boom, another 50% off. Unfortunately, 50% off, plus 50% off, doesn't add up to free, but it might as well have been. I walked out of the store with two really nice shirts for $6.25 that were previously priced at $50 each. Now that's favor.

Pat and I have experienced the Lord's favor whenever we have bought used vehicles. The price was always fair and they always ran better and lasted longer than we needed them to. The only time that wasn't the case was when we convinced ourselves that we needed to make a decision and got in a hurry. The car still ran well, but we hated driving it because we knew we could have done better by anticipating that He would show us precisely the one to purchase.

Favor also comes in other packages such as people introducing you to others that are able to connect you with people who are necessary for your journey and purpose … and for you to do as much for them.

Part of anticipation is the pursuit of peace. Do you need to make a decision? Pursue the one that gives you peace. Need to make a choice? Choose the one that provides the most peace, not necessarily the most benefit. When you are in doubt about peace in the process, doing nothing is also an option. If you follow peace, then you can anticipate God showing up somewhere in it.

Hebrews 10:35 "Cast not away therefore your confidence, which hath great recompense of reward." (KJV)

The one thing that blocks anticipation for us is our continual battle with rejection. This generally comes from childhood, but can also be the result of issues as an adult; rejection, betrayal, robbery, etc. A series of them in life can result in an alteration of our expectations to include rejection. I have an internet acquaintance who was scammed in a real estate transaction. She didn't lose her property but did lose most of her savings as a result of it. She wants to move on with her life but she's held in check because she can no longer build up enough trust in people to allow a realtor help her get the equity out of her real estate so she can move on. Neither can she trust God to help her again because she blames that loss on Him.

If you are in a similar boat, then the course is simple for you. Find someone who can help you deal with the loss, the betrayal, the rejection, etc. so that you can once again have hope that the giver of good gifts has not disqualified you from receiving them.

Here's another one that has struck me recently about not seeing what is before us. On January 15th, 2017 representatives from 75 nations convened in Paris to make plans to make two states out of the existing borders of Israel so that the Palestinians would have a state. Part of what was in the balance was the control of Jerusalem. Currently, Israel claims Jerusalem as their capitol, although all government offices and activity is located in Tel Aviv. The Palestinians are demanding that no Palestinian state can be declared without Jerusalem being its capitol.

Personally, I doubt this will ever come to fruition for several reasons, not the least of which is our experience of having spent three weeks in Jordan and Israel in December 2016. I can tell you what Jerusalem would look like within 90 days, and you wouldn't ever want to go there. Angry people will never produce anything of value, only discord. Their situation is never their fault.

Every word of scripture concerning the end times declares that the nations of the world will descend on Israel in an effort to wipe the

Jews off the face of the earth forever and remove the nation of Israel from existence. The meetings in Paris of January 15th of 2017 were the beginning salvos of that war, meaning that all the events leading up to that point are now in the process of being fulfilled somehow before us.

This means that now, more than ever, there is a requirement for each of us to be fulfilling the mandate in Matthew 6:32-33,

> *"(For after all these things do the Gentiles seek:) for your heavenly Father knoweth that ye have need of all these things. 33* **But seek ye first the kingdom of God, and his righteousness**; *and all these things shall be added unto you."* (KJV)

Interestingly, those much-ballyhooed meetings in Paris devolved into utter chaos, with round after round of recriminations for non-participation by the 'major' world powers coupled with an inability to come to an agreement on anything. Not one consensus of any kind could be reached. The representatives of each of the participating countries all went home, each blaming the other for the lack of progress.

God laughed.

8 Ownership

I posed this question earlier, "If you have been granted permanent membership in THE club (The Kingdom of God), but choose to operate under another club's rules, are you a real member of THE club? or are you just an imposter?"

Obviously, there is room for argument here, but let's stay with the metaphor. The Kingdom is not a club, but it is somewhat like a club from our Western perspective. People gravitate to it because those in it connect with the King and are granted membership on that basis, and yet it is far different from a club because its members are from totally varying nations, ethnic groups, education, on and on. And the King of the club can boot you out of it without you even knowing it. Note the language in the following verses ...

> Matthew 5:3 "*Blessed are the poor in spirit, for* **theirs is** *the kingdom of heaven.*"

> Matthew 5:10 "*Blessed are those who are persecuted for righteousness' sake, for* **theirs is** *the kingdom of heaven.*"

> Matthew 13:41 "*The Son of Man will send his angels, and they will gather* **out of his kingdom** *all causes of sin and all law-breakers,*"

> Matthew 19:14 "*... but Jesus said, "Let the little children come to me and do not hinder them, for to such* **belongs** *the kingdom of heaven.*"

If you picked up on the terms used in these verses from the Book of Matthew, the Kingdom has ownership; Jesus and the Father can boot out or accept anyone He chooses, and yet those who are chosen also seem to have ownership of it as well. This is a function of relationship.

> Matthew 25:34 *"Then the King will say to those on his right, 'Come, you who are blessed by my Father, **inherit** the kingdom **prepared for you** from the foundation of the world."*

One cannot have an inheritance without having become a relative, either through blood, adoption, or marriage. Ha! In the believer's case, it tends to be all three, although the marriage has only been scheduled.

> John 1:12 *"But as many as received him, to them gave he power to become **the sons of God**, even to them that believe on his name:"*

One also cannot have an inheritance without the demise (death) of the owner of that which is to be inherited, in this case, Jesus the Christ. I think it's really funny to muse on the trick Jesus played on satan when he died. First, as a result of Jesus' death, we were given a massive inheritance. Then rather than stay dead as satan expected, Jesus rose from the grave, kicked satan's butt and now sits at the right hand of the Father in Heaven (The King of the Kingdom) to help you and I kick satan's butt again and again. Now that's some inheritance, eh?

There is also apparently "rank" in the Kingdom as well, or another way of saying that there is a specific order to the Kingdom.

Matthew 11:11 *"Truly, I say to you, among those born of women there has arisen no one greater than John the Baptist. Yet the one who **is least** in the kingdom of heaven **is greater** than he."*

Matthew 5:19 *"Therefore whoever relaxes one of the least of these commandments and teaches others to do the same will be called least in the kingdom of heaven, but whoever does them and teaches them will be called great in the kingdom of heaven."*

Apparently, rank is linked to instruction in Kingdom things, or discipleship, and a specific aspect of it.

Matthew 7: 21 *"Not everyone who says to me, 'Lord, Lord,' will enter the kingdom of heaven, but **the one who does the will** of my Father who is in heaven."*

When we lived in Asheville, NC (the origin of the Cherokee Trail of Tears) I did a lot of land cleansing at the direction of the Lord. For those of you unfamiliar with the term; standing in as an intermediary before the Lord asking for forgiveness on behalf of those whose sin had defiled the land. I knew that at each location many people before me, many of whom were famous in Christian circles had prayed over other issues there or in the area. I was only there to do MY part and pray only what Holy Spirit asked me to pray.

I did so with full faith and confidence that if I did what I was supposed to do, and others did what they were supposed to do, that the Lord's will would be done in the entire region. And if His will was being done then His Kingdom would come. (Matt 6:10) Doing as the Lord bids is a distinct Kingdom honor, even if there is a personal price paid for doing it.

The Kingdom of God looks relationally like a family. For the household of the family to operate successfully, especially if it's a large family, each member has to faithfully discharge his or her responsibilities by accomplishing the chores they have been assigned in order to make the household run. Ownership in the Kingdom entails functioning in your specifically assigned role and using your gifts, skills, talents, and abilities, in the process. Because "no man is an island" each of us must support those around us as well as complete our chores so that the family as a whole accomplishes its goal. Being self-absorbed is not a Kingdom virtue.

9   *Non-competitive*

For many of you, this will seem a bit farfetched because it would seem to preclude a great deal of backyard fun, as well as rob us of all manner of enjoyable sporting activity. That's not the point, for being competitive takes us to places we've never been before and requires better things of us that we have not understood were actually in us. The two ends of the spectrum are the ones we need to guard against; having to win to prove our self-worth, and hating to lose because it might declare who we are.

Every one of us is familiar with the child that pouts excessively or throws a fit if they don't get what they want. Disappointment is a natural element of life. Witness Jordan Spieth's 12th hole implosion at the 2016 Masters Golf Tournament at Augusta, Georgia. At the 11th hole, Spieth was winning by 5 strokes and looking at a winner's check close to $2,000,000. Two holes later he was trailing the leader by four. In a closing interview, with his voice cracking, his words were, "This one will hurt. It will take a while." Greg Norman suffered a similar collapse on the back nine in 1996 that gave Nick Faldo the crown. He said it took him the better part of six months to get over what happened. "Even though I was at the peak of my career and playing better than ever, I questioned myself almost every day trying to get to the bottom of what happened."

The thing about both of these two individuals is that they have actual lives, not cardboard ones. They are not trying to prove that they are somebody through the sport of golf, they are just trying to do their best with what God gave them. Their worst days playing golf didn't destroy them because neither of them was afraid of failure, and neither of them is defined by golf. It's just something they chose to play – and for both of them, play is still the operative word. Yes, it is played very seriously, but for them, it is play nonetheless.

Although both of these men play (Spieth) or played (Norman) professional golf for a living and both have made a lot of money doing it, neither of them would say that they are competing against others but against themselves, which is why they are all able to remain friends and celebrate each other's good fortune. That same observation has been made by numerous top-shelf professional golfers. This is possible because their value as men is not determined by how well they play golf.

The Kingdom does not recognize competition. It does recognize striving to become like Jesus, to bring justice for the widows and orphans around you, peace and safety to those who are being, or have been abused, feeding the hungry and caring for the dying, etc. Competition carries with it the idea of being better than another in a contest of some specific skill. The Kingdom is all about doing your best, (demonstrations of excellence) as the golfers noted above are well aware, not to prove that you are better than someone else, but to see how proficient you can become. Neither competence nor legitimacy comes from winning a contest, it's more the result of winning an internal battle against the resistance from within and without.

So if you hate to lose, and winning is everything to you, then you have a couple of issues that need to be sorted out, or if fear of failure blocks you from being all you have wanted to be, lay it before God and find someone to help you sort it all out. For either of these will hinder your entrance into the Kingdom, as well as your ability to remain in it.

Let's look at this from another perspective. Are you easily able to rejoice with someone who wins or receives a gift of something valuable unexpectedly? Or are you jealous of them and silently complain that it should have been you? If this is the case don't continue to live in denial about it. Get some help, or forever stay trapped in the Matrix of the system of the world.

10 Mercy

In the Kingdom, Mercy always triumphs over judgment. Not so in the world. When someone has been grieved or offended they want their pound of flesh – immediately. And yet The Lord's Prayer of Matthew 6:9-15 is clear that we should pray for forgiveness (mercy – Matt 9:13) toward those who have hurt us and to top that off, we have to ask forgiveness of those whom we have harmed. It further states,

> Mark 11:26 *"But if you do not forgive, neither will your Father which is in heaven forgive your trespasses."*

> Matthew 5:7 *"Blessed are the merciful: for they shall obtain mercy."* (KJV)

> Exodus 33:19 *"And he said, I will make all my goodness pass before thee, and I will proclaim the name of the LORD before thee; and will be gracious to whom I will be gracious, and will show mercy on whom I will show mercy."*

We have received mercy therefore we have the resources to give mercy, a major element of the Kingdom.

> Matthew 10:24-25 *"The disciple is not above his master, nor the servant above his lord.*
> *25 It is enough for the disciple that he be as his master, and the servant as his lord.*

Giving Mercy is a function of our ability to love in difficult circumstances, or to love those who are intentionally making themselves difficult to love. When we are betrayed, or stolen from we want instant justice; punishment for the offender and restitution for our personal losses. My first encounter with theft in Africa was met by the Lord's Word from *Proverbs 6:30,*

> *"Men do not despise a thief, if he steal to satisfy his soul when he is hungry;"* (KJV)

Unfortunately, I was much more interested in applying Exodus 22:1,

> *"If a man shall steal an ox, or a sheep, and kill it, or sell it; he shall restore five oxen for an ox, and four sheep for a sheep."* (KJV)

> 1Chronicles 16:34 *"O give thanks unto the LORD; for he is good; for his mercy endures forever."*

Westerners are all about law and justice. When those are paired together Mercy will never find an occasion for expression. Law and justice are helpful to provide order for a society but is never useful in the context of relationships in the Kingdom. In order to be able to appropriately apply mercy one cannot live in accord with the world's system. The two are totally incompatible. Here's why. In the Kingdom, there is no such word in its vocabulary as "failure." It does not exist. In the Old Testament is it recorded as,

> Psalms 145:14 *"The LORD upholdeth all that fall, and raiseth up all those that be bowed down."*

> Proverbs 24:16 *"For a just man falleth seven times, and riseth up again: but the wicked shall fall into mischief."* (KJV)

Then in the New Testament Jesus obliterates the limitation completely when Peter comes to him asking how many times he has to forgive a man who fails him daily,

> Matthew 18:21-22 *"Then came Peter to him, and said, Lord, how often shall my brother sin against me, and I forgive him? till seven times? 22 Jesus said unto him, I say not unto thee, Until seven times: but, Until **seventy times seven**."* (KJV)

If there is no such thing as failure in the Kingdom of God, then where does our concept of fairness through the application of Law and Justice have a place to stand? Following the rules, especially if they are of our own making, never served to produce a relationship. In the Kingdom, we willingly choose to follow the directions of the King, not rules. So the law no longer exists. We chose to live by love in response to the love of the King who is love.

To those who have chosen to no longer remain faithful to the system of the world, abandoning law and order to adopt living by love seems to be terribly risky. What do we do with those who chose not to? You have to understand that we are talking about a superior set of principles that pertain only to those in and of the Kingdom. Those who choose to love can embrace it. Those who love the world will never subscribe to them and will even be hostile to them all their days. Your choice or inability to move from the world into the Kingdom will prohibit you from ever understanding why one will produce peace and the other will always bear the fruit of conflict and discord – the only thing it can produce.

11 There is A Reward

There is a reward for living life in the Kingdom of God, but it does not come from the world. This is one of the biggest producers of disappointment for believers that there is. This is because we have always had our hope and trust in the system – "If I do right everything will be right." What we unconsciously think is, "If I do right (according to the system I know) then everything will be right (because the system will honor my efforts.)"

The Kingdom of God is sufficient unto itself. It does not depend on the world to reward you for things the King of the Kingdom wants to bless you with or give you because of what you are called to do. But by the same token the Kingdom with not reward you, or regard you, for being a hot-shot in this world.

> *James 1:7 "Every good gift and every perfect gift is from above, and cometh down from the Father of lights, with whom is no variableness, neither shadow of turning."*

Just because scripture uses the term "gift" doesn't mean a periodic transfer of something valuable such as on your birthday, or at Christmas. The promise is held for us in Matthew 6;31-33,

> *31 'Therefore take no thought, saying, What shall we eat? or, What shall we drink? or, Wherewithal shall we be clothed?*
> *32 (For after all these things do the Gentiles seek:) for your heavenly Father knoweth that ye have need of all these things.*

33 But seek first the kingdom of God, and his righteousness; and all these things shall be added unto you." (KJV)

In other words, God has got all this covered for you – everything you need to sustain life – delivered directly from the fully stocked warehouses of the Kingdom. If He has to make the world's system deliver it to you, or another believer, or a kind un-believing benefactor, or just create it out of thin air, He will. It's coming to you … provided you are seeking the Kingdom (v.33).

The world tells us that it's all on us to make it happen, which causes us to worry. Verse 34 expressly says don't give any energy to worry, it produces nothing but more of the same. The King of the Kingdom says, "I got this. Go on about your day and be a blessing to somebody."

In Genesis Chapters 12, 14, 17, 18 and 22 we read that Abraham was Blessed to be a blessing and that all the nations of the earth would be blessed through him. Part of that blessing was that through Abraham the family of the Jews would be born, and through the line of the Jews, Jesus would come.

Also in the book of Hebrews, he is called the father of faith. So you and I are both inheritors and beneficiaries of the blessings of Abraham, but being a joint heir with Jesus Christ, we too are blessed to be a blessing. And this was the plan of the Father all along, that you and I would live our lives worry-free in the Kingdom and thereby provoke the people of every nation to jealousy (Romans 11:11).

The Kingdom, just like its King, carries its own reward.

Now I want to give you something to counter the notion of many conservatives that this viewpoint is wrong because it fits the American consumer desire to have it all without measure and is non-spiritual.

Jesus said this in Mark 10:23 *"And Jesus looked around and said to his disciples, "How difficult it will be for those who have wealth to enter the kingdom of God!"*

Jesus is not out to make you wealthy, but He is determined to cause you to enter rest from striving, and that's what that section of scripture is really all about. The world is totally against the Kingdom of God because it requires you to have faith in God's ability to save and keep you, to provide for you, to heal you when you need it, to protect you when you can't protect yourself, and to care for you in old age when you can't and no one else will. The world says everything is up to you. So if it is recorded that Jesus said,

Luke 12:31-32 "Instead, seek his kingdom, and these things will be added to you.

32 "Fear not, little flock, for it is your Father's good pleasure to give you the kingdom."

… and He was just talking about all the "stuff" that you and I need to survive this. It isn't about conspicuous consumption at all. It's one of the enemy's plans to get you to fear wealth. Jesus wasn't against wealth. He was feeling sorry for those who so feared lack or were trying to create value for themselves, that making money was their sole pursuit in life.

The world isn't jealous of poor people. Poverty is not considered a blessing in any society anywhere on earth. The world does not want what they have because it means that they would have to follow their god as well, which apparently isn't at all beneficial. The world's god promises money, fame, power, and sex; all of which requires a form of slavery. Our God is armed with good and perfect gifts, which are His great desire (pleasure) to bestow on those who follow Him. The greatest gift is a peace which the world can never supply.

There is another aspect of this equation; You can only impact the lives of those who are in your individual sphere of influence. If you are married with 2.5 kids (national average) and making $45,000 annual (slightly above the national average), you are not going to be living in a gated community hob-knobbing with the country club set. Does that mean that God is not interested in the wealthy? Not at all. Some folks are "called" to minister to the wealthy so they can address their particular needs, which someone making $45K/year has no grid for. As much as he might like to fill that role, this will not be filled by the pizza delivery guy handing out tracts with the pizza.

And while I am on the subject of wealthy people, if you are in ministry in any form, quit judging the wealthy for not supporting "your thing." The vast majority of them are generous in areas you know not of. Charity is not dead. The reason they choose not to back your project is that too much of your appeal is about you, and what you want to do, not the needs of the helpless. Yes, you mention the needy in your appeal, but these folks are spiritually sensitive as well and they can smell an ulterior motive a mile away. So check your heart before you make an appeal to the wealthy, or better yet, have the Lord check it for you. The motivations of your heart may be hidden from your conscious awareness, but they are wide open to the Lord, who even protects wealthy believers.

12 Sowing and Reaping

By its title, you are ready to skip this chapter figuring that you already know what it's all about. If you have been a believer for any length of time this topic is not new to you, but there are so many things we have been taught, had modeled to us, even expected from us by others in the world that you would think that sowing and reaping is all about you and what you have to do ... more rules and regulations. Nay, Nay ye skeptic. This chapter has as much in it to rejoice over as the last one.

First a bit of my personal testimony. I have already stated that I came to the Lord a fairly early age, about 9 as I recall, or so the inscription in a red Bible my father gave me following my Baptism declares. I don't ever remember Lordship being one of the topics taught or being discussed in the church as a kid – and we went a lot. In fact, every time the doors opened. My Dad always seemed to be a Deacon or the Chairman of the deacons of every church we were a part of, so he was there to both open and lock the doors any time there was a meeting. So I got dragged to an awful lot of meetings, including the ones where they argued, fussed and fought over the color of the paint for the hallways, whether the new toilet seats for the women's restroom should be round or oval, and whether they should change the offering receptacles from a woven basket to nicer wooden plates (the ones that had green felt in them like the top of a pool table), and on and on it went. Sometimes the discussions would grow rather intense and one of the men would storm out, whereupon they would adjourn, only to repeat the whole sordid thing again in a week or two.

Well, when I left for college, I chose to leave behind my father and mother, their church, their religion and all that went with it. For the next fifteen years, I lived life pretty much as I pleased, never darkening the doorway of another church. A tour of duty in the military rounded off some of the sharp edges; then holding down a full-time job while also enrolled full time in college taught me a few more valuable lessons. There were successes, but plenty of failures.

By the time I arrived at the ripe old age of 32, I was divorced, had joint custody of 2 young children, I had just lost a job and I was for all practical purposes, a functioning alcoholic. My brother, who also lived in the same city, had been prodding me periodically, to come to church and one Sunday evening in late early December I did. I knew I was at the end of my rope and there was nothing else to do but let go. So as I stood in an aisle in the back of that massive church sanctuary in Houston, TX and I made the most bizarre "confession of faith" you could ever imagine, "Lord, if you can do anything with the mess I've made of my life, have at it."

Not exactly the kind of faith-filled declaration that your momma would have hoped for, but it was raw, real and oh so sincere. I was done trying to run my own life the way I wanted to. It was now officially "in the ditch" and there was nothing I could see to do that would change that.

What does that have to do with sowing and reaping? My life was the seed I sowed. It was the only thing I had left and I sowed it in the only way I knew. (John 12:24, Mark4:26-27) That day I think I really entered the Kingdom because a King isn't a King unless He has something to rule and reign over.

Within a very short period of time, the fruit of that decision began to blossom in my life in very rapid fashion. Within seven months I was married to a wonderful woman who is still the joy of my life, I had a new and much better job in another State, and so both of us could delightfully say that "All our Ex'es lived in Texas." Then my relationship with the Lord began to grow in ways I could not have imagined.

The point of this story is that so long as you are doing your own thing, and not the Lord's thing, you are all the resource of blessing you are ever going to have, which in my case wasn't much. That's the way it is when you do your own thing because you think God is just a crutch for the weak. You just have no clue who the real weakling is. When you are engaged in the Kingdom, the options become endless.

You see, there's an actual (even physical) exchange made when you invest yourself in the Kingdom, or when you invest any of your assets in the Kingdom. This doesn't mean that money will miraculously appear in your bank account if you donate your spouse, or drop the kids off permanently at a monastery. However, if you invest your funds in a kingdom ministry (as directed by God) you will find that your personal business will prosper financially. Kingdom money (no matter how small) invested in Kingdom endeavors produce kingdom fruit you can hold in your hand. Favor and opportunities that were previously unavailable to you will also suddenly become a common occurrence.

We have some friends who started a ministry several years ago in Nicaragua. Almost from the beginning, they were supported by people who were not believers, but who were interested in providing humanitarian aid for disadvantaged people. Over the years God has significantly blessed these individuals financially. The Kingdom blesses those who bless the Kingdom.

Somebody is going to get their undies in a bunch if I don't mention the wages of sin in the context of sowing and reaping. So here it is. If you continue to do dumb, harmful, self-destructive stuff, sooner or later you'll reap the rewards of your stupidity. (See the beginning part of this Chapter.) This is true whether you consciously do it or not.

Most of our dysfunctional (even sinful, anti-social and anti-relational) behavior is an unconscious response of self-protection against experiencing additional emotional or physical pain. Self-protection is not a Kingdom concept. So even in simply trying not to experience additional pain, we open ourselves to the consequences of using worldly protection mechanisms against emotional and spiritual attacks, which will never work. You always reap the fruit of what you have sown.

As an acquaintance of ours, Eric Hurtgen says, "The way the kingdom comes, IS the kingdom that comes."

Now, there's another element that needs to be expressed and that is the fact that occasionally the Lord will ask you to do something that seemingly has no temporal reward associated with it. This includes pretty much all intercession on behalf of individuals, healing prayer in the marketplace, evangelism of strangers you encounter along the way and acts of land cleansing, which I love to do. Will there be a reward for all of that at some point? Who knows? I assume there will be, but when the Lord puts it on your heart you are simply compelled to do it without a promise of reward. I have described it in the past as, "It would be harder not to do it (be disobedient) than to just do it." Besides, around my home growing up when momma asked you to take out the trash, it really wasn't a request, in spite of the fact that it was phrased that way. Honor always does what is needed, as well as what's right.

If your heart is really in the Kingdom then being rewarded for your efforts is not central to your motivation. So the idea of not receiving an immediate or even future compensation for your meager sacrifice isn't in your heart anyway. You do it because you love Him and love people – or as also in my case also, you love the land. To be sure, the scripture promises a reward for the "deeds done in the flesh" (Matthew 6:1, 6:18, 9:41) as we will experience on Judgment Day. So yes, that can be a motivating factor, but that isn't what we strive for as Kingdom citizens.

13   *Servanthood*

If you have been a believer for any length of time this topic is not news to you either, but there are so many things we have been taught, modeled to us, even expected from us by others in the world that this is a tough one to wrap our hearts around. American ideals are far from servanthood. In fact, to many, it spells weakness and is the absolute antithesis of success in life that we have been raised on. We have heard people trying to motivate others to say, "If you're not a leader, you're a follower." That totally demeans the roll the vast majority of us engage in because a company with all leaders will accomplish absolutely nothing.

> Luke 22:24-27 *"And there was also a strife among them (the disciples), which of them should be accounted the greatest.*
> *25 And he said unto them, The kings of the Gentiles exercise lordship over them; and they that exercise authority upon them are called benefactors.*
> *26 But ye shall not be so: but he that is greatest among you, let him be as the younger; and he that is chief, as he that doth serve.*
> *27 For whether is greater, he that sitteth at meat, or he that serveth? is not he that sitteth at meat? but I am among you as he that serveth. (KJV)*

I believe that this concept is partially at the root of the failure of the American church to radically impact the world at large. We have effectively bought into the thought that leaders don't serve, and even if we've embraced the idea of servant-leadership we really don't know what it looks like and therefore can't model it to anyone over any length of time.

The last few years we have become acquainted with numerous foreign missionaries and missionary organizations in Africa and Southeast Asia. We spent both the Spring and Fall of 2015 and 2016 in Mozambique, Africa ministering to long-term missionaries and a bunch of IRIS Harvest School Staffers. On our first trip, it took my wife and me about two weeks to come to grips with our attitude about superior American ways. Part of it is being faced with the rampant grinding poverty there reinforced by multiple generations of it. Like all Westerners, we had the basic presumptive attitude that if you (Africans) would do as we Westerners do, then poverty would soon be a thing of the past.

The reality is that it probably takes at least three to four generations to effectively deal with the poverty mentality of the single group of people you are ministering to. That cannot be accomplished without men (not just in the general sense) being a major part of the daily training and discipling work of altering an entire culture. And those men have to have servant hearts in order to effectively strike at the very foundation of the dysfunction of less developed societies where might makes right and corruption is a way of life.

Native Mozambicans threw the Portuguese out in 1975. The country erupted in Civil War in 1977 – tribe against tribe struggling for power over the entire nation. The damage that was done to the economy and infrastructure when the vast majority of Portuguese left the country was completed by the civil war which raged on from 1977 to 1992. There has been a great deal of political maneuvering since then with at least one of the three major factions in disagreement with the ruling powers. These factions are organized largely along tribal lines, each generally in control of one-third of the nation from South to North. In early 2016 one of these factions in the central part of the country armed themselves and began periodically disrupting commercial traffic on the main north-south highway by shooting at and disabling trucks carrying supplies. Again, the strongest arm rules. That method is typical in Africa because those in power are among the few with access to wealth and power, which is the foundation of the corruption that is so widespread in virtually every country in Africa.

The servant-leadership spirit of Nelson Mandela never made it out of South Africa to Mozambique in the form of additional native leaders, and consequently, it has never been effectively modeled there, nor apparently has it survived very long in South Africa. Consequently, both countries are ripe for another revolution as each is on the verge of economic collapse (as of this writing.)

In the Kingdom, you get promoted by promoting others. You get promoted by serving others; by holding the interests of others above your own. (Philippians 2:3-4) Exercising competitiveness actually robs you of the Kingdom.

To complicate matters, Mozambicans are stuck in a dangerous mental quagmire; it is a vicious stew comprised of resentment and unforgiveness for offenses from 500 years of presumably oppressive Portuguese Colonial rule (even though none of the folks complaining about it were actually alive at the time), distrust of people from other tribes, rising suspicion and racial animosity toward all westerners, coupled with the orphan, victim and poverty spirits from generations past. The depth of the quagmire is made even worse by the national disease of corruption on virtually every level of government and particularly with the local police force. Getting out of the county through local airports without a fine is basically a crap shoot.

This makes being mentored in any arena very difficult with a governmental environment that is Marxist and a peculiar form of communism is the order of the day and where the government is Big Brother in the truest sense of the word. When you throw in significant influence from religion, witch doctors, and superstition, the society and commerce become a big mess. Corruption then rises to a whole new level.

This impacts relationships on all levels and severely complicates the long-term conduct of any Christian ministry because all these wind up as part of the lives of local ministry employees that have to be addressed in the context of their existing culture.

Our time in areas where there have been high levels of poverty has required us to re-evaluate our own personal values. There is a temptation to believe that your ways are also God's ways, particularly if you are blessed financially, which comparatively speaking, every American is. The reality is that if you have managed well using the principles of the world, and have been blessed by God at the same time, it takes some very keen insight to see that your presumptions about the Kingdom are actually out of whack with reality.

One issue I had was with time. I tend to be very observant about appearing for appointments in a timely manner and I pride myself on always being on time for appointments, in fact, I am generally early. Initially, we had been given a schedule to meet with people in one-half hour increments and those schedules are woven in and around the ministry school's class schedule. The problem is that Mozambicans don't own watches. They don't even own calendars. So classes don't really have a schedule, they just go till they're done. That was aggravating to me. I was raised to believe being on time was a matter of showing respect to the one(s) you are to meet with.

Mozambicans don't care about time because their entire society is completely event oriented. When there's an event scheduled they will go early to see and visit with their friends, afterward they may go visit with local extended family, do some shopping, whatever. So the whole day is consumed by a single event. And they love it that way.

I was complaining to the Lord about the situation and He said this to me,

*"The American understanding and application of the gospel are based upon a foundation of European interpretation – at the time supposedly the most civilized society on earth. But history well shows another story. It operated on a similar set of values shared by the balance of the civilized world. Americans believe that they are the "pinnacle of civilized society" because they personally don't hurt anyone, or persecute anyone, when in reality anytime you are trying to **force** people (any people) to adopt your values, that is exactly what you are doing.*

There are things of great value in the Mozambican culture that need to remain in it. They are not to be uprooted and supplanted by your American idealism. Do you want all Mozambicans to live under the same stress of productivity you live under? I forbid it! It is slavery. To compound their survival slavery with performance thrown in is insanity. I love these people. You do not. So do not insist that your ways are higher than theirs. Yes, there is much that you can teach them, but there is much you could learn from them as well."

One of the admirable things in their society is their uncompromising dedication to family and community. A missionary informed me of this characteristic through something he had learned which illustrates this point perfectly. If a member of a western church strikes up a relationship with a Mozambican pastor of a local church, he will eventually come to visit. When he comes he will naturally see many things that could be improved with the application of western resources, namely, cash. The westerner sits with the pastor and declares that his congregation would like to help this community by supplying money to accomplish project XYZ. They agree on a plan. The pastor leaves and sends the money needed.

Sometime later the westerner visits the pastor to find out how things are going and to see firsthand the progress made on project XYZ, only to find that the project is not only not finished, but the funds have been exhausted. The westerner asks the local pastor to give him an accounting of the funds disbursed and finds that the pastor's nephew received 15% of the funds due to a medical emergency, and he is shocked. The westerner accuses the pastor of theft, which is a major surprise to the local pastor because in his society the needs of people, and especially family, come before projects when resources are available.

The westerner goes home vowing to never trust another African and the local pastor refuses to deal with another arrogant westerner because they are compassionless and too preoccupied with money to even want to truly understand and appreciate their needs.

The westerner feels justified in his beliefs and yet never spent enough time with the locals to understand why a health emergency ranks so high on the "I-gotta-take-care-of-this" list. It is because life expectancy is so short in Mozambique. For males it is 52.6 years, for females, it is 54.1 years, per www.indexmundi.com. Healthcare is effectively limited to the amount of cash you have. If you have an accident, you don't get treatment unless you can pay for it. Generally, there is really no such thing as preventative care because of its lack of affordability, not to mention availability. The local hospital in Pemba lacks much of the equipment and medications that are normally available in any neighborhood clinic in America.

In our western societies, the care for the injured and infirm has intentionally been handed off to institutions and professionals to handle because of our dysfunctional relationship ability, and our sense that 'specialists' can do a much better job. It has been expanded to care for the elderly when it used to be the sole purview of the extended family.

That's what performance and perfectionism have brought us to. We're way too busy.

So we throw around the words "family" and "community" abundantly without ever really understanding them, nor any intention of learning what they mean. My thought is that if you were to randomly test people in a coffee shop by asking them to list ten things that are *Benefits* of Community and *Responsibilities* of Community in five minutes, I would bet that the Benefits list would have an average of five entries and the Responsibilities list would have an average of one and a half entries.

These are not exactly Kingdom ways, but it is the way of the world in Mozambique. One cannot impact the culture there without understanding it first. In order to understand it, you have to immerse yourself in it. An occasional visit and reading about the country on Wikipedia aren't gonna get it done. Even King David said, "*I will not give to the Lord that which costs me nothing.*" Kingdom expressions will cost us something.

14 Specialization

To live together separately, as we often do here in America, was never God's original design, but was man's invention, especially in this age when the average male waits till age 28 to get married, while the average female waits until she's 27 to wed. This is the first time in recorded history where less than 50% of the population is married.

I use the term 'specialization' specifically because it perfectly describes the solution man, invoking the wisdom of this world, has assumed to prescribe as a cure-all for a common problem. There is an age-old adage that says, "Work expands to consume all available time." When I worked as a product manager and a systems integrator we well understood that "Every task, in every project, takes as long as it takes." (The word "guesstimate" comes to mind.) We certainly understand the truth of that viewpoint, but some might express it differently, by quoting one or more of Murphy's Laws, "During an important project anything that can go wrong, will go wrong." or "The number of things that will go wrong will be in proportion to the importance of the project." Or perhaps more personally, "There are just not enough hours in the day to get done what I need to do."

So humanity's response is to divide and conquer. Whoever is deemed to be more adept, or better equipped or educated to handle a given task takes (or is assigned) responsibility for completing it. Very practical, but not necessarily very rewarding.

But because it makes perfect sense from a practical perspective, specialization is born and remains a fixture of modern life. Consequently, specific roles are accepted and life-altering activities are entered into. All elements of our society buy into it and a fully formed functional caste system is forever established, relegating significant elements of mankind to roles people think they are "better suited for" functionally, or worse, roles they can never escape.

The system of the world then takes advantage of the concept of specialization as politicians build a tax and control system around it by requiring specialized activities be certified, which requires licensing fees and taxes to support other government 'recognized' specialists to help monitor and regulate it.

Above is a fairly recent photo of some Muslim refugees walking to reach the final objective, to live safely in a European country. There are 7 men and 1 woman. Observing it a bit closer, you will notice that the woman is walking barefooted, accompanied by 3 children; she is carrying 2 of them. Therein is the problem, none of the men are helping her, and all the men are wearing shoes because in their culture the woman represents nothing. She is only good to be a slave to the men. Specialization run amuck.

Mind you, God didn't design the Kingdom this way. Granted, women do a better job of conceiving, carrying and birthing babies than men do, but just because that sort of physical design specialization works for us in the reproductive arena doesn't imply that it's a universal rule for all remaining human endeavor and societal interaction.

The fundamental problem engendered by specialization in the developed portions of the world is that in our performance-oriented society, function implies identity; *"You are what you do."* If you don't believe it, just go to any large group gathering of men who are strangers to one another and begin to introduce yourself to others. The common response will most often be, "Hi, my name is Bill and I'm a _____." The more important the "work" function is deemed to be by your social circle the more personal importance it presumes the performer is to their company, as well as to society as a whole.

Therefore, title and function have culturally imputed value. Cognitively we can say that's not true, but that's how we act particularly when it comes to corporate titles, educational degrees, board memberships and country club memberships.

What we have collectively done is to come into agreement with the world's system and its way of doing things. It automatically attempts to change your entire focus toward something you are not, but also causing us to see others other than who they are.

Because we buy into that valuation system, value and personal worth become ascribed to things that cannot bring lasting personal fulfillment. For instance, on the surface, it would seem that the products of perfection and excellence would be pretty much identical. But perfectionism drives you where excellence compels you. In time, perfection will stomp out all creativity you have managed to hold on to while pursuing excellence will enrich it. One is actually a counterfeit of life calling, while the other is the natural expression of it.

The unintended curse of our specialization is that it forces us into man-made roles and culturally defined strictures, which in many cases definitively and intentionally denies significant characteristics which God purposefully installed in us for the benefit of all mankind, whether we are male or female. What it tends to do is reduce all life equations to produce one answer; Is it practical? Is it productive? Or more to the point; Can it help me make money and therefore be esteemed in our culture?

Because there are several seasons in life, there are a myriad of opportunities which arise to keep us separated, including the natural seasons of life; school days, getting a job, building a career, establishing a marriage, building and nurturing a family, putting kids through college, empty nest, retirement (noted as an extra-Biblical concept) and our twilight years.

There are personal seasons of maturity; Being cared for by parents; learning to care for yourself (dress, feed, cleanse); learning to care for others (wife, husband, children, and elderly parents); eventually learning to care for a community. These are the natural steps of maturity. However, the system of specialization has demanded that some of the responsibilities of these seasons have to be farmed out to folks 'more capable than you.'

In our Western society, most of these have been both well defined and refined by the individual roles culture has established for us simply based upon whether we are male or female, whether we are husband or wife.

Further, we are all taught to specialize by every influence in our society (read: the system of the world). It is now practically unthinkable for someone going into the field of medicine to desire to be a general practitioner. There's no money and no future in it. One must enter into an increasingly narrow field of medicine in order to thrive. Even GP's themselves will give you a referral to a specialist at the first hint of diagnostic difficulty, the reality being that the more people you see the more you make. (It's all about retiring the school debt, you know. Hence the emergence of socialist thought of a free college education in American politics.)

God's original design for unity has already been stated. I refer you now to Romans 11:29: *"For the gifts and calling of God are without repentance."* God has not changed His mind. His design criterion for you has never changed. He intentionally designed a specific assignment for you and equipped you to complete it. Regardless of the mistakes we've made, the paths we've chosen, or refused, or the culture we live in, He's never changed His mind.

So what's the answer?

What is necessary for each of us to do is to engage the Lord and ask Him to;

a) Reveal to us where society or our own choices have relegated us to something other than what He created us for?

b) Where have we given in to "natural selection" or specialization and adopted a "role" rather than pursuing what He created us to do?

c) Where have we (I) made decisions that required me to settle for less purely for practical reasons?

d) Where have I chosen to become a specialist for financial reasons and consequently have forsaken huge chunks of my life that were once fulfilling?

e) Where have I accepted belief(s) about myself that have relegated me to much lesser roles than I should be giving myself to?

Don't be afraid of what He will show you. Remember, *"Fear not little flock, It is your Father's good pleasure to give you the Kingdom"* is actually in the Bible. (Luke 12:32) You haven't been disqualified, only delayed.

15 unity

The book of Ephesians, Chapter 4 encourages us to keep the *"unity of the Spirit"* and to continue to press in *"till we all come into the unity of faith."* It is preceded by, *"With all lowliness and meekness, with longsuffering, forbearing one another in love."*

Now I know that this letter was written almost 2,000 years ago to a church close to the mouth of a river in what is now northern Turkey. I would also assume that as in any church there were sold out Christians, there were also average Christians and there were nominal Christians and there were a few non-Christians as well. (Or pre-Christians as some preferred.) So Paul's direction to them to be *"longsuffering, forbearing one another in love"* was meant to be toward their fellow Christians, and well as to those who were the pre-Christians among them. In order to do that we must intentionally practice unity by becoming largely un-offendable.

Unity is in short supply these days. In America, it is a scarce commodity because we are so quick to adopt an independent spirit and call it a virtue. We are quick to adopt the media birthed images of John Wayne, Chuck Norris, Bruce Lee and such lone crusaders such as Superman and Batman. That is the epitome of the spirit of this world.

The Apostle Paul writes in every letter, even as he did to the Romans;

> *"8 First, I thank my God through Jesus Christ for you all, that your faith is spoken of throughout the whole world.*

*9 For God is my witness, whom I serve with my spirit in the
gospel of his Son, that without ceasing I make mention of you
always in my prayers."*
(Romans 1:8-9)

He writes that he is proud of those whom he serves and has
taught; he compliments them on their faith, their deportment, their
charity, their struggles, as well as their care for others. Yes, he chided a
few as well because they were getting out of order with food and drink,
as well as dedication to the things he had taught them. His goal was
they should help one another in maintaining order and dedication to
the Lord. Peer pressure is a good thing. And yet we seem to prize our
independence fiercely.

When people post their dreams on social media it usually
includes an isolated cabin way off in the mountains on a lake or stream,
hidden away from civilization. But then later, when they want to get
away from it all where do they say they want to go? To the beach,
along with ten million other people.

There is a somewhat schizophrenic side to humans. We hate to be
surrounded by 1,000 people and yet we can't bear to be without them
either. We join clubs because we want to be with people who like the
same things we like. We love to retreat in isolation but couldn't bear to
live outside a noisy, congested, claustrophobia-inducing city. We only
want unity on our terms.

Unity is not thinking the exact same thing and saying the same
thing. Scripture points out in 1 Corinthians 12:4-7 that we are all
different, consequently no two people are going to do the same thing
the same way, neither will they see the same issues the same way. That
does not mean that they are against one another. They are just
different.

The last two Presidential Administrations have brought our country to a place of division close to that experienced during 1860-61. 2016 was a Presidential election year that disclosed just how divided we are. We saw relentless hecklers and protesters disturbing campaign speeches, then refusing to stop even though the election was over, as though their protestations would overturn the selection.

The rampant fear that someone you disagree with will sit in the Oval Office has propelled a rather large compliment of the lunatic fringe in this country to a level of frenzy we've not previously witnessed. There is no longer room for discourse. To protest at the President Elect's post-inauguration party made no sense whatever. Everyone knows you are mad about it, the only thing it proves is that you are still mad and want everyone to know it. Point proved, but to what effect? The same spirit that is driving politics is loose in the Body of Christ as well.

Let me give you an example. An acquaintance of mine posted on Facebook that he was dining at a specific restaurant here in town. My wife and I eat there only about once every eight or nine months because we have seldom had a great meal there. We have had to send back a number of items because they were either not done, or were not cooked to specification. I even had to send a side salad back once because it was frozen solid. So we go there just frequently enough to remind us why we don't go there regularly.

The mistake I made was to comment on his post, "XXXXX, The home of Mediocre." His reply was, "I showed this to the manager, He asked who it was that wrote it. I told him it was just some religious jerk I knew." I don't know how we jumped from a comment about restaurant quality to my 'religious' character. I am aware of a few food critics who are jerks, but the fact that we had only previously interacted briefly twice still has me puzzled. But the bottom line is that I violated my grandmother's code of conduct; "If you don't have anything nice to say ... shut up."

The choice to divide is easier than overlooking minor indiscretions, or giving someone the benefit of the doubt and choosing to believe that someone simply misspoke. Our reaction to being 'attacked' is often to become politically correct – make sure you don't ruffle feathers, or step on toes, when the Bible admonishes us to speak the truth in Love. (Ephesians 4:15)

The Kingdom is about unity, so there is a requirement to both speak and respond differently than the worldly norm. We need to be personally aware and in control of our heart attitudes toward people and ideas that cause us to react in worldly ways and yet never back down from speaking the truth when it will edify.

The news is full of reports of people who were offended by something someone said, or an idea they declared that is diametrically opposed to theirs. The presumption is that they have a right to live their life un-offended. Good luck with that. It's obviously not a Kingdom value. Scripture tells us,

> *"If it be possible, as much as lieth **in you**, live peaceably with all men.* (Romans 12:18)

That tells me that there's an awful lot of stuff I just need to let slide, and if someone offends me my question should better be, "Why does it offend me?" rather than demanding an apology, or popping 'em one upside the head. We should give people the benefit of the doubt, and think the best rather than judging them and telling everyone else what we think of them. People have good days and bad and if we are all judged by what we do and say on our bad days we would have a lot of bridges to repair.

We must become virtually un-offendable in order to keep our Kingdom focus. In order to do that, we have to reign in our emotions and dump our offenses, (real and imagined) at the feet of Jesus. Then spend time with Him finding out what got touched and if it was appropriate.

16 Some Personal Background

My wife and I were raised by parents who were Christians, all born ten to twenty years after the turn of the century. Their parents, lived through the Depression era (1928-39) and WWI (1914-18), the Korean War (1950-53), and WWII (1939-45). They learned well the hard lessons that those times brought. It established priorities for them; some good, some bad. Our parents lived through the domestic sacrifices brought on by WWII, the Korean War and the social upheaval of the Vietnam War. Both my father and I served in the military during wartime; he in WWII and me during the Vietnam conflict.

Our parents were raised in a time that firmly believed that marriage was exclusively for a man and a woman, and it was a permanent arrangement, the man in the marriage was the head of the household, and raising kids was a job for two people. They both equally understood authority and responsibility and the need to teach their children the same.

Our parents had autonomy in making decisions in the realm of their work and in household authority. But when it concerned significant family decisions; those decisions were made as a couple, preceded by prayer. They were couples who had joint checking and savings accounts, with both able and expected to sign on them. They also shared a relatively similar set of social and religious values.

So when Pat and I got married we had a great deal in common simply by virtue of our common upbringing. We both held management jobs in separate industries and were frequently promoted. We both made good money and never even discussed whether we would have separate checking or savings accounts before or after we married. In our minds that was just what married people did naturally. We merged our accounts when we returned from our honeymoon.

Thereafter, when we made decisions we consulted one another; we usually discussed, prayed about and considered them together. We never gave thought to doing it any differently. In brief, we started our marriage by acting as a unified pair. We have always done much the same with our offerings and monetary gifts. Unity in marriage looks like honoring each other.

A good friend of ours was married for almost 30 years when her husband died of cancer. He handled all the money. He gave her cash to buy groceries and the beginning of each week, otherwise, she had no knowledge of what came in or went out. When he died she had to pick up everything, including closing down his business without any knowledge of where to look for information, who they owed, nor how much they owed. When she sees him in heaven, I imagine he's going to hear a great deal more than, "Hi honey! Long time no see."

Honoring each other by making each other a part of everything in your life is an expression of love, relationship and trust, that at least in our case, was understood to be a fundamental element in a marriage which was passed down through our respective families of origin, beginning with our grandparents and perhaps even further back than that. The issue of the need to initially adopt a position of unity was ingrained in us and got us off on the right foot. This is partly because we see marriage as a partnership and a house divided cannot stand.

Many people we work with today didn't have the privilege of growing up in a situation where they could learn trust by having other family members model it, who always had their best interests at heart. Consequently, they have always felt the need to be independent in order to protect and promote themselves. Many have also never had a model for parental unity that was nurturing, protective and beneficial.

Often, this lack of unity is the source of difficulty when attempting to find a common life calling. If there is no unity in these other areas of marriage the potential is not great that they'll achieve it in ministry either.

There is one other point I would like to make while I'm on the subject. The reason I felt it important to give you a bit of our family background is that we seemed to have come to entering into unity quite naturally. Loving someone certainly makes it easier, but many have never really learned how to love, and consequently, have been introduced to what trust looks like in that environment. If you never had it modeled, it is a tough step to take, especially if your partner in previous relationships was economically dysfunctional. But if your background is similar to ours it is a much easier transition.

Now this may sound a bit preposterous to some of you, but it is reality; many of the values passed down to us from our grandparents and parents are actually practical expressions of everyday Kingdom principles.

Unity in marriage between spouses is a Kingdom principle. (See Proverbs 33) So is unity among brothers and sisters, in the Lord and otherwise; along with authority and the proper assumption and discharge of personal responsibility. (You can't have one without the other.) As is honesty and integrity. So is providing continuing security, safety and income for your family (1 Timothy 5:8). And so is the continuous instruction and discipline of children.

Our fatherless society has created an entire generation of self-absorbed orphans who know nothing of the keys to successful living, and it is the primary reason we are experiencing the perverse relational climate nationally. Everyone is dead set on providing for themselves or getting someone else to do it for them. Everyone else be damned!

If any of this is even similar to the way you think then finding your life's calling is going to be nigh unto impossible. I don't mean to say that the Lord will never reveal it to you or that you will never find it. What I am saying is that so long as everything is about you, you will never be able to see beyond your own need, your own wants ... or your own pain and disappointment when these things don't materialize in your life. Consequently, you will never see the problem you were made to solve. Your heart will never be pricked sufficiently to pay a price to find a solution to somebody's crippling issues. And your eyes will be blind and your ears closed to the crying need of others, even if the Lord Himself parades it before you.

In the words of a far greater author/poet than I, John Donne, "No Man Is an Island."

> *No man is an island,*
> *Entire of itself,*
> *Every man is a piece of the continent,*
> *A part of the main.*
> *If a clod be washed away by the sea,*
> *Europe is the less.*
> *As well as if a promontory were.*
> *As well as if a manor of thy friend's*
> *Or of thine own were:*
> *Any man's death diminishes me,*
> *Because I am involved in mankind,*
> *And therefore never send to know for whom the bell tolls;*
> *It tolls for thee.*

So please get over your narcissistic self and join the rest of mankind. If you know you have unresolved issues from childhood and you struggle from time to time with nagging emotional pain, seek help to resolve those issues so that you can get on (and into) with the life

God has designed for you. This includes anger, lack of trust, and an independent spirit. If you really want to live, you really have no other choice.

That is what I and countless others have dedicated our lives to; helping folks resolve the deep issues of life that keep them from experiencing the fullness of relationship (complete and total unity) which exhibits trust in all matters, a life lived from the heart rather than from the head, and for many an opportunity to really feel loved for the first time. I think I can safely say this on behalf of all of those of us who have dedicated our lives to helping others, our lives have become so much fuller and richer for the effort.

That's another expression of a Kingdom principle. It is better to give than to receive. (Acts 20:35)

17 Being an Ambassador

2 Corinthians 5:20 *"Now then we are ambassadors for Christ, as though God did beseech you by us: we pray you in Christ's stead, be ye reconciled to God."*

Strong's Concordance provides a definition of the Greek word rendered 'ambassador' in this verse is G4243 Πρεσβεύω, presbeuō, pres-byoo'-o; from the base of G4245; to be a senior, that is, (by implication) act as a representative - be an ambassador.

Webster's 1833 Dictionary defines it as; *"A minister of the highest rank employed by one prince or state, at the court of another, to manage the public concerns of his own prince or state, and representing the power and dignity of his sovereign. They are also called ministers."*

If indeed we are in it, we, as either an individual or a couple, are ambassadors, ministers and representatives of a superior kingdom sent to a foreign one (in which we physically reside) to demonstrate the superiority of that heavenly kingdom in comparison to the rules, regulations, laws and principles of this earthly kingdom and those that rule over it. Since our citizenship is elsewhere, we choose only to follow the laws of this realm as dictated by the laws of our own, choosing to practically demonstrate to the citizens of this realm the ascendant supremacy of our own, and the dominance of its benevolent sovereign head.

This is achieved by acting in accord with your of purpose and assignment in every aspect of life, naturally as dictated by the King or the Kingdom. Your ministry is not what you do, it is how you live. If how you live is not first and foremost characterized by love and the pursuit of a deep and abiding relationship with God then there is ample reason to question which kingdom you are actually living in. Now we would always choose to say that we are doing the best we can, but the reality of how our lives are characterized is in the hands of others who are not swayed by the nobleness of our grand intentions, but are judged on the basis of our actions. Often there's a big difference.

Over the years I have listened to, loved (even tolerated), cried with, laughed with, lived with, played with, given food to, paid bills for, given advice to, encouraged, trained, chastised, taught, given cars and vans to, vacationed with, ordained, married, buried, and just hung out with all kinds of people. Dozens of people have lived with us from time to time. We even had another family live with us for three years, which was one of the best experiences of our lives. Our lives have touched a lot of others. I am not saying that from a place of pride, although I am proud of it, I am simply saying that I (and my wife) have consistently shared our lives with others and gave them the best we had along the way. In the early days, it may not have been much more than hospitality, but it's what we had because that's what was in our hearts.

I remember wanting to buy a set of Interpreter's Bibles years before all this stuff was digitized, which as I recall was about 12 to 14 volumes, each about 2 to 3 inches thick, and around $50 each. I got a call from the owner of a Christian bookstore I frequented on the west side of town, saying that he had a set someone wanted to sell. I drove out there and found the books to be in great condition, but they were being offered by a pastor who was selling them to help pay off his wife's medical bills. I paid him for the entire set of books but told the store owner I couldn't take them as the pastor probably needed them far more than I did; they were still his.

The store owner told me later my simple act of generosity spoke volumes to the church board and the congregation; that a total stranger cared more for the plight of their pastor than they did. In response, they paid off the pastor's debt entirely. The unity that it produced sparked major life in the church and it was growing again. If you say you love, then you have to put your money where your mouth is.

I am certainly happy that that's how it all worked out, but it wasn't what I intended. In my mind, it was just a small gift to a guy who needed some help. God obviously had other plans in mind. I was just doing what I thought was right for a person who was struggling; sharing my life and resources as an Ambassador of another, more benevolent and powerful kingdom.

By a simple demonstration of the superiority of Kingdom principles, the lives of those involved in that rural congregation were impacted and their response to it changed them. As Ambassadors of the Kingdom, we have within us access to the solutions to the most perplexing problems the world faces today. It doesn't come simply by study, for there is no course to take. It comes by living the Kingdom life with The King in the midst of everything you are involved in.

Remember, **you can't export what you don't first have.**

Now, having said all that, I have to remind us all that we are Ambassadors of Love and Relationship, which is our chief aim, as well as our primary weapon. It is who our King is. He doesn't have love. He is love. Consequently, His subjects must choose to love, strive to live from love, daily espouse love and continually act like lovers, regardless of the circumstance we face. And you can only do that in the context of relationship. Often the charismatic expression of the church has elevated gifts, particularly the power gifts, as the primary and even final expression of the Kingdom. Failure to major on love has unfortunately brought a measure of pride and spiritual arrogance that is hated equally by the world, other religious traditions, and our King.

The election cycle of 2016 has effectively drawn a line in the sand between liberals and conservatives in America. In their victory, many in the church and wanna-be Kingdom dwellers have embraced a self-righteous separatism, consequently forever linking them to the more legalistic and radicalized segments of religious whackos. (Read that as racists, homophobes, and woman haters.) This has resulted in the establishment of an impenetrable wall between them and the other half of Americans.

The only way that this wall is going to be breached is by individual Christian Kingdom minded people beginning to intentionally and transformationally love their neighbors into the Kingdom, one-on-one, and one-by-one as a true Ambassador is supposed to.

We have collectively gone and hid in the church, locked ourselves away with people who are like us, who share our values, who are roughly from the same socio-economic backgrounds and attend the same church. Three-quarters of American churchgoers, black, white or Hispanic, never associate outside the church with people of another race, or socio-economic group because they do not share the same values. It's human nature to gravitate to others who are like you. But we cannot be Ambassadors for Christ if we choose to only associate with people who are already Christians. As Kingdom dwellers, we need to change our habits and start fishing in the water where the fish are, not asking them to come to our pond where we would like them to be.

One element of this behavior is the mistaken belief that because non-Christians don't share our "Christian" values that they don't share any of the rest of our values either, and therefore hanging with them couldn't be anything but a struggle. My God, they might offer me a doobie and a beer! Then what would I do?

The reality is that all human beings generally share the same set of desires. We all want to be loved, respected, spoken well of, don't care to be around people who are always negative, we like those who are kind and considerate and have a sense of humor. We all like folks who share and will show up if we need help. There is more commonality there than we believe, and yet we hold them at arm's length simply because they are different than us.

As Christians, we throw the word 'community' around a lot and even believe that we have it in the context of the church we attend. They all seem to be nice people, and even greet us when we show up and ask us how we're doing when we see them. But the grim reality is that our familiarity with them is pretty much limited to facial recognition. We don't even know if we have anything else in common with them other than we attend the same weekly meeting ... and we dare call that community.

I dare say that if a random group of your church acquaintances were asked to write down a list of the benefits of being in community and the responsibilities associated with being in community, you would get a lot of blank stares.

If that is the extent of your 'community' then you need to face the facts. You not only don't have a community but you're hanging with a bunch of folks who either don't know what it is or who are so insecure that they don't want it and wouldn't know what to do with it if they had it.

An ambassador of the Kingdom is inclusive, hospitable and open to people who are different than they. They would no doubt be highly surprised, but wouldn't necessarily be offended if a neighbor offered them a doobie and a beer during a Summer afternoon visit. One or both of the two offerings might be refused, but both would be welcomed because that sort of an offer is an open invitation to friendship.

Several years ago I spent an afternoon with an evangelist who spent much of his time taking groups of people to Argentina with the expressed intent of winning an entire city to the Lord in 30 days or less.

His method was simple. His large team would fan out over the village or city, going house to house, asking the occupants a very simple question; What do you need that only God could do?

The entire team would meet at the end of each day, share what they'd heard and pray for every need. Then go back to each dwelling they had visited at the end of each week to see what God had done. If there was no report they would keep praying for them as a group. Over the course of a month, the residents were stunned to find that God was answering prayer in their behalf all over their city, on their street, among their neighbors and friends, among family members, even in their own household. The evidence was massive and unmistakable. God cared. And so do these people who know Him.

These were simply ambassadors of the Kingdom going about the business of calmly introducing them to the caring superiority of the King of the Kingdom that they represented.

The question then is this ... Can you do at least that much for your neighbors?

One of the things that surprised the team members was how quickly real community was formed following their demonstrations of kindness. Groups began to form to see who else in their neighborhood needed help. They somehow formed bonds that were never there before. They learned to pray – together. Nominal Christians began to seek the Lord, people were getting saved and having all kinds of encounters with God. Word of more miracles began to circulate and more neighbors wanted to join. Their mutually expressed care and concern for one another broke down long-standing walls, repaired relational fractures and obliterated differences which isolated them from one another. All this happened because a team of Ambassadors of the Kingdom chose to bring the practical good news of the Kingdom to a people who desperately needed some.

Look at 2 Chronicles 16:9 and ponder it a while. You meet the qualifications.

18   What Do You Want?

Back in 2001 Pat and I were trying to figure out what God's will was for us in moving from the Atlanta area to Asheville, NC. I had experienced a real 'out of the box' introduction to Asheville and felt that we were to relocate there. At least I hoped we would; anything to get out of the rat race that is Atlanta's traffic congestion. Following that initial introduction, I had sought the Lord consistently for about six weeks, with no response whatsoever. Then one evening at the end of a long work week, following an evening ministry session with a local pastor, God caught me by surprise, asking, "**What do you want?**"

I was stunned by the question "What do you want?" because that didn't fit my theology. I felt that He was supposed to tell me what to do and I'd go do it. That's the way I had been taught and had always understood it to be. Then He said, "**Slaves think that way, not sons. What do you want?**" I knew it was an important question that demanded more than a quick answer, but I was so caught off-guard by it that all I could think of as a response was, "I'll have to get back to you on that."

I spent the next couple of weeks considering my response. We think that we know ourselves well and that surely any response we make would reveal a great deal of the truth of what we want. That's not necessarily true. I can tell you ten things I would like to have right now, but none of them would I pay a heavy price to have. They are just things I'd like to have.

The question that was asked was much deeper and much more important than, 'What would I like to have?' What did I really want? The personal search of my soul and spirit for a truthful answer was the whole point of the question. It wasn't until much later that I realized the wisdom in the question; I needed to know what I wanted. God had already packed it in there somewhere and many of life's wounds, choices, and troubling circumstances had tried to cover it up, even disguise it. It was a big deal to have to honestly answer that question because I somehow knew that the answer would play a large part in forming the balance of my life.

Knowing what you want out of life (or perhaps what you want to do with your life) provides these somewhat profound benefits.

- It tends to focus all your energy and your attention.
- It determines the price you'll pay for getting what you want.
- It fixes vision for you and establishes where your personal will is focused.
- It determines what you will give significant chunks of your life in exchange for. You're going to spend it on something! What is the most valuable thing you can get in the exchange?
- It determines what you won't quit on when there's a titanic struggle and things don't look good.
- It determines what you'll sacrifice for, what you'll plan and prepare for.
- It prioritizes what you'll work for and pray for.
- It fixes what you'll dream about and talk about.
- It determines what you won't give up – if you'll finish well.
- It establishes purpose.

- Ultimately, it forces you to think about what sort of mark you want to leave on this world by your presence here? And even gives input into how you want to maximize that presence.

In the final analysis, everyone needs to know the answer to the question; *"What do YOU want?"*

That doesn't mean that you don't consult God in the process, because you're going to need help to discover the gem you're looking for, but eventually you will need absolute clarity regarding what you want and whether it squares with what He wants? That's when complete clarity comes. Having clarity can mean the difference between sticking with it when other opportunities present themselves or bailing when times get tough. Both of which you'll experience.

Again, Proverbs 16:9 says that a man plans his way, but the Lord orders his steps. God is the only one who sees the end from the beginning (Isaiah 46:10) and knows how to get you there.

But perhaps the most significant thing about the question, "What do you want?" is the fact of personal choice. God intentionally created us with a free will. That free will can only be exercised by making choices. We have the choice to choose not to follow Christ. We have the freedom to choose if we will submit to His will and we also have the freedom to choose to do something with our lives that is only meaningful to us, even if it means nothing to anyone else. We can through personal choice become someone we were never meant to be. Granted, it probably won't be very fulfilling in the long run, but nevertheless, unlike any other creature in the universe, we have that choice. We even have the choice not to choose, and just go with the flow, taking whatever comes along.

We also have the choice to be more than average; to break the bonds of mediocrity that fear of failure tries to enforce. You have a choice to attempt to fulfill every dream, every wish; be a hero to yourself and those around you. And my, oh my, does the world ever need heroes. Today more than ever.

Matthew 6 tells us to 'seek first the Kingdom of God.' How do you know that what you are pursuing (or what you want) is part of it, or in accord with the Kingdom of God? Or for that matter, how do you judge the balance of the pursuits of your life on that scorecard? The only safe manner to make that call is to engage God in determining if indeed your pursuits are in accordance with that of scripture and the will of God, then make a choice to continue or not.

Jeremiah said Chapter 17, verse 9,

"The heart is deceitful above all things, and it is desperately sick: who can know it?" (RV)

I think this is what King David had in mind when he said in Psalms 139:23-24

"Search me, O God, and know my heart: try me and know my thoughts: 24 And see if there be any way of wickedness in me, and lead me in the way everlasting."

He was referring to the fact that we often do not know the motivations of our own heart, its secret desires being hidden from us by protective mechanisms we unconsciously erect in response to pain and woundedness. David's only recourse was to go to God and ask Him to show him what he could not see … the unconscious thoughts and motivations of his heart. Such action should be our model.

The path to maturity is a process of consistently trying to make the right choices, a compilation of small but good decisions, along with making the most of your mistakes by correcting the thought processes that got you there. That's where the balance between "What do you want?" and "Father, what do you want?" is struck. You must learn to know your own heart, all the while leaning on the One who really knows it, as well as the path ahead in order to make certain that the two converge.

Here's another verse that plays into this equation;

Daniel 10:12 "Then said he (Michael, one of the chief princes of God) unto me, Fear not, Daniel: for from the first day that thou didst set thine heart to understand, and to chasten (discipline) thyself before thy God, thy words were heard, and I am come for thy words." (KJV)

This is part of the process of maturing in the things of the Kingdom. We need to understand that we don't know what we don't know and that that ignorance can be destructive to us and those we love. And that it can delay us in becoming who we were created to be and sidetrack us from the things we were created to do.

All that to say this ... every heart desire we have is not from the Lord. We must know which are mine and which are his. I love to sail and have had many small sailboats over the years. Sailing is a wonderful sport as well as a great leisure activity, but is it a must-have for Kingdom living? No, it isn't. But do I still want another one? Yes, I do. The key is to know the motivations of your own heart. Sometimes we have to discipline ourselves in order to allow a Kingdom-oriented response to override our fleshly desires.

Shortly after we moved from Asheville, NC to Campbellsville, KY in 2011, the Lord surprised me again during a worship service by asking, *"What price will you pay to do what I've called you here to do?"* When He said it I instantly knew what He was talking about (or thought I did); a level of personal discipline I have never wanted to embrace. Again, it is perfectly scriptural.

We must count the cost at each new level of our personal destiny. There will be many such decisions along the way. But we also needed to know exactly why He called us here. One without the other doesn't mean much. If you don't know where you're going any road will lead you there. Scripture says that God is not the author of confusion. (1 Corinthians 14:33)

Unfortunately, we humans often make totally wrong assumptions, as I did that day, that what He was talking about was a new foray into personal discipline; ie. concentrating on dieting and exercise. Sometimes we blow right past the Ask/Seek/Knock thing. It wasn't until a few months later that I realized He wasn't talking about reducing my waistline. He was actually wanting me to enter a new level of personal discipline in teaching. You see I have always much preferred to fly by the seat of my pants when teaching; Notes, What Notes! I don't need no stinking notes! But in the last 24 months …. let's just say that … I am learning to find a brand new and lasting appreciation for teaching from detailed notes. (But I tell ya, Old non-Kingdom habits die hard!)

19 Retirement

I want to briefly address the subject of retirement. First of all, retirement is not a Biblical concept. It originally referred to a period of time very late in life during which a person could not continue to work due to advanced age, along with some age-related infirmity that prohibited it; a season which needed to be prepared for along the way. There was no point in an individual's life where he or she became non-active. If you ever lived on a farm you know why.

Our Western culture has artificially advanced the official date of "advanced age" to a time in life where sufficient resources are available such that daily work activity was no longer necessary and one could spend the balance of his or her life in leisure pursuits; do that which they previously had no time for.

The problem with that is that retirement then becomes the ultimate goal in life and all others are held at bay by it, including the Kingdom. It further requires that all competing activities are subservient to it, potentially meaning that Kingdom life must be delayed until there are sufficient time and resources to accommodate it; making the act of retirement anti-missional and anti-Kingdom.

I certainly understand and appreciate the belief system, but the vast majority of men, particularly those who gave themselves to this viewpoint did so in such a fashion that they could not properly reorder their lives when vast amounts of discretionary time became available. The original goal was sufficiently powerful to have made Matthew 6:33 a vague concept achievable only by serving the goals of the institutional church (at best), hence stripping it of any real power in an individual's life and forfeiting the real purpose for which they were created.

This is why I believe that the discovery of our life's Kingdom calling is so necessary for us given the weight of the previous Chapter on mission. It is absolutely necessary for Kingdom-minded people! (the remnant: Romans 11:5). If properly identified and established it will give us a track to run on for our entire lives whether we are employed or not and ensures that the precepts of Matthew 6:33 stay prominent to the end, allowing us to finish well.

Further, Jesus said that he came to give life and life abundant. So engaging Matthew 6:30 becomes a fulfillment of the purpose of Jesus coming to earth in bodily form; the fullness of emotional and spiritual life. That is precisely what was robbed from those who gave themselves exclusively to careers rather than the Kingdom. There you have it; the key to life abundant and all the fulfillment your heart can hold.

Another element of 'retirement' that is somewhat more diabolical is the fact that focusing on and preparing for retirement tends to completely consume us. Certainly not consciously, but because it is a specific long-term goal it can demand specific decisions, establish priorities and orders behavior that take precedence over all others, even God's direction. By asserting itself in this manner 'retirement' has become a god; the idea being that I'll have sufficient resources and time to do what I want to do, i.e., complete independence. This is more evidence of the relentless pressure of our totally narcissistic society and the credence of its values which tend to hold Kingdom priorities at bay.

Don't misunderstand me to say that planning for the future is not a necessary Kingdom value. If you don't aim you are going to miss the mark. It's just that when we establish retirement as the 'ultimate goal' of our working lives and the process of storing up the resources to fund it, we forfeit the best that God has for us. Kingdom pursuits and preparing for retirement are not mutually exclusive pursuits but so many people view them that way, as though one conflicted with the other.

This is where the rubber of love and relationship parameters of Kingdom citizenship meets the road. If these are not somehow integrally expressed through the execution of your career, it won't be expressed during retirement either.

I am simply urging you to restore a balance to your priorities so that your entire life is productive for the Kingdom, not just the part that you think you can more properly dedicate to it because you no longer have the requirement of making a living hanging over your head. That in itself is a gross violation of Matthew 6. Chose to seek first the Kingdom and I can assure you that all the rest of this stuff will take care of itself.

There is another aspect of retirement that isn't always obvious and that is the function of it as a reward for having been forced to work for 30 years just to live. Retirement is the point many have been looking forward to as an expression of freedom from the grinding responsibility to provide.

Many people are fortunate in that they were able to make a living doing what they were born to do. But for those who were trapped in a career because it paid them too much to quit and do something that they really wanted to do, retirement is like a breath of fresh air and a splash of sunlight after having lived the life of a mole. The problem is that the new-found freedom wears off all too quickly because folks became so accustomed to the harness they wore for so many years. Without one they feel purposeless.

The failure to recognize that we had become slaves to responsibility and performance to the point that after a while a feeling of being valueless sets in which makes us oblivious to our value outside the harness that was our dictator. The freedom that was once so prized feels formless and void; without meaning because there are no expectations, no deadlines, no goals, outside of keeping the lawn looking good. Under those conditions, freedom can be a tough taskmaster because it makes no demands.

If you consider all the prominent people mentioned in the Bible there is one thing that is common to them all, regardless of what strata of life they came from; they were folks with a cause, a reason to live, people of action. God did not create us to sit around and do nothing. It is the big causes that we give ourselves to that bring meaning to life; especially the ones that require much from us.

Having something bigger than yourself to be involved in is the key to maintaining a vital relationship with God and others; the impossible always ensures connectivity. The small stuff we can handle on our own without Him or anybody else, which is where we typically miss the boat entirely.

Besides, God never calls you to something you can do all by yourself.

We moved from Atlanta, GA to Asheville, NC and spent 11 years there. During that 11 year period, we lived in nine different homes. The majority of them were land cleansing and healing assignments; I pursued the Lord and local information from history books, spiritually determined the issues and engaged the Lord for cleansing and re-establishment of the blessing of the land. On occasion when that assignment was done we would lose interest in staying there. On other occasions, the Landlord decided when we needed to move on. Either way, the assignments were always interesting.

One such assignment involved a house that was a 3,500 sf two-story home, built onto a kitchen that had been constructed in 1863; the balance was completed in stages by 1892. (see www.worleyplace.com) The home originally stood on 400 acres on the west side of the French

Broad River on one of two parcels in a land grant to the family by the King of England in 1764.

The home had enjoyed some updating along the way, none of which included insulation. Our first two weeks in the home in December cost us $400 in fuel oil. We resorted to heating the two-story structure via a wood-fired stove and thanks to the gracious offering of firewood from Fred and Miriam Hayes we remained financially solvent. Before bed, we would stoke it to near red-hot, moved the furniture away from it, then flipped a coin with two others who lived with us to see who would get up in three hours to stoke it once again. A midnight visit to the bathroom ensured that you were wide awake when you returned to bed. Great fun.

Investigation of public records revealed that several members of the family had served in the office of Sheriff of Buncombe County numerous times over the previous 150 years, with all the usual you scratch my back, I'll scratch yours, good 'ole boy stuff going on. Some of their actions would raise some eyebrows today probably as much as it might have back then. Interestingly, the family also owned a tobacco warehouse for about 100 years on the south side of old Asheville near the Swannanoa River up until about 1988 or 89. Both of these facts played heavily in the prayers for land cleansing. However, once the prayers were prayed we immediately lost interest in staying in the house and started asking the Lord for something else.

On some occasions boredom is actually God calling, saying I've got something else for you to do. Boredom or lack of motivation is generally one of the signs my wife and I pay attention to because it says change is typically in the wind. It's not a universal sign because we have to have pay attention to our attitudes and make adjustments like anyone else. There have just been so many such incidents that boredom, or perhaps a better term might be "a restlessness," has become one of the telltale signs that signaled we're about to have an adjustment in ministry. Such are the mysteries of Kingdom motivation that God uses to signal a change in scenery.

If you were driven to keep working at your current job for several more years because you felt you had to in order to be able to retire, your life would be miserable when the message of boredom or restlessness came to call. If you will not be saddled by the Kingdom, something else much less accommodating will saddle you.

I have also written a book entitled, *"Finishing Well"* (available on Amazon) that I would refer you to because it ties in with the topic of retirement and the concepts in it are all in line with Kingdom Principles, which probably ought to be part of this book as well, but you really didn't want to have to wrestle with a five pounder.

20 What Does All That Mean?

First of all, *"he who does the will of my Father"* (in Matthew 7:21) is juxtaposed against the following statement, *"depart from me … you workers of iniquity."* (Matthew 7:23)

Obviously, we can grab most of the import of that. If we are not doing the will of God, we are doing the will of somebody else. The clue is the use of the word 'iniquity.'

Webster's 1833 Dictionary yields this definition of the word iniquity; *"Injustice; unrighteousness; a deviation from rectitude (rectitude; In morality, rightness of principle or practice; uprightness of mind; exact conformity to truth, or to the rules prescribed for moral conduct, either by divine or human laws. Rectitude of mind is the disposition to act in conformity to any known standard of right, truth or justice; rectitude of conduct is the actual conformity to such standard. Perfect rectitude belongs only to the Supreme Being. (The more nearly the rectitude of men approaches to the standard of the divine law, the more exalted and dignified is their character. Want of rectitude is not only sinful but debasing.)"*

Iniquity comes from a couple of sources: our conformity to the teachings of this world, and conformity to the 'understood' doctrines of our generational line. For example, we may attempt to control or manipulate our circumstances to avoid being hurt again. But that would simply be personal re-enforcement for someone who originally learned it at the feet of their father, mother, and grandparents by watching them.

So what Jesus was saying in Matt 7:23 (paraphrased) was, "depart from me those of you who choose to model the systems and practices taught to you (passed on by your parents) by the god of this world, rather than my father's."

Do you realize the way you balance your checkbook is inherently evil, simply because it was taught to you by the system of this world, which is the realm of the enemy? It may well be efficient and effective for the task at hand, but it is only that way because it is aligned with the system of this world.

Doubt it? I can prove it to you. What is the basic premise behind balancing your checkbook? One of the basic philosophies behind balancing your checkbook is founded in quantifying how many resources you have remaining versus what it takes to do what you need or want to do. In essence, it is fear based. I need to protect myself from the penalties.

According to Matthew 6, Ephesians 3:20 and Philippians 4:13, we have all the resources we will ever need to do what we've been called to do, including what we will wear, eat, drink, as well as where we lay our heads. Now, we know that we are to be good stewards of what He's given us, so we need to keep an eye on what we have, but the way of this world is to focus on what you have (typically small) in the face of what you need (typically large).

This has the effect of magnifying the power of the 'taker" over the power of the 'Giver.'

Another major reason people chose to balance their checkbook is to avoid over-drawing their account and risk having it closed. Call that good stewardship if you like, but that motivation is essentially founded in fear. Fear is not in the vocabulary of the Kingdom of God. It is one of the chief ingredients in all worldly strategies.

I rest my case.

Romans 12:2 *"And **be not conformed to this world**: but be ye transformed by the renewing of your mind, that ye may prove what is that good, and acceptable, and perfect, will of God."* *(KJV)*

Let me add one more observation. Matthew 6:30-33 was spoken to the population of a strictly agrarian society; farmers, shepherds, and fishermen. Their needs were simple but the promise covered them all. They didn't have cars or gas, phones, car insurance, housing mortgages, bank accounts or internet bills to be concerned about. However, these things are ordinary elements of our society today. God is not oblivious to those additional needs simply because they were not specifically enumerated in the Bible alongside what you will wear, and what you will eat and drink.

So what's the point? Unless we hang around Jesus a lot (Ask, Seek and Knock) we will never see the small, iniquitous understandings and patterns of thought that cause us to adhere to the systems of this world, which are inherently anti-Christ and anti-Kingdom ... and anti-us. Without it, we will remain completely conformed to the systems and thought processes of this world (Romans 12:1-2). We may be busy doing many good things, which are roundly applauded and extolled as virtuous by the good people of the world, but if we are not closely connected to Him and consequently doing what He directs us to do, we are simply working iniquity to the best of our human ability.

I know what you're saying to yourself right now: Didn't you just say that God asked you *"**What do you want?**"* Now you're saying, *"**Do what He directs you to do**."* Isn't that a bit contradictory?

No, not at all. Do you remember the verse that says, *"Delight yourself in the Lord and He will give you the desires of your heart?"* (Psalm 37:4 KJV) It is my considered opinion that God actually installed your heart's desires in you at birth, if not before. The consequence is that your heart's desire will also be His desire, as you turn it toward Him He will cooperate in seeing that your dreams are accomplished. So there really is no conflict at all.

The problem arises when we don't know the dreams, desires or motivations of our own heart, or we are not acquainted with Him well enough to find out what it is that He for wants for us. That's one of the principal reasons God asked me, "What do you want?" I desperately needed to commune with my own heart. I needed to know what was in there that I was not intimately connected with.

> *"Stand in awe, and sin not: commune with your own heart upon your bed, and be still. Selah."* (Psalm 44:21) *"Shall not God search this out? For he knoweth the secrets of the heart."* (Psalm 4:4) (KJV)

On occasion, our own subconscious iniquitous belief systems can be the blockage that keeps us from being able to know the reality of the message of our own heart, as well as His.

We cannot do this without Him. That's the fun part about this whole exercise; walking it out with God in the center of it all. It really is all about the unfolding development of an organic unscripted relationship with Him; you discovering you while you discover who He is. This is truly why He said, *"I will never leave you nor forsake you."* (my paraphrase of Matthew 28:20b) It's fundamentally all about relationship.

21 The Will of God

Matthew 7:21-23 *"Not everyone who says to me, 'Lord, Lord,'
will enter the kingdom of heaven, but the one who does the will
of my Father who is in heaven.
22 On that day many will say to me, 'Lord, Lord, did we not
prophesy in your name, and cast out demons in your name, and
do many mighty works in your name?'
23 And then will I declare to them, 'I never knew you; depart
from me, you workers of lawlessness.'*

We have read this series of verses numerous times in our
Christian lives and it can honestly be quite frightening to be doing the
best that we can, and yet still missing the mark, then reading it again.
We are all too aware of our faults and failures. But this isn't about our
performance or how we measure up. There are several things that
Jesus is saying that are inter-related and confusion will come if they are
all not understood together.

In verse 21 we see the title given to Jesus by those approaching
him is "Lord, Lord." The word LORD is defined as; From κῦρος kuros
(*supremacy*); *supreme* in authority, that is, (as noun) *controller*; by
implication *Mr.* (as a respectful title): - God, Lord, master, Sir. The
distinction is whether the speaker is saying it strictly as a title for Jesus
because of their mental assent to his place, or are they saying it in
recognition of who He has become by virtue of their experience with
Him? There is a huge difference.

The fact that you and I cognitively understand who Jesus is and can correctly address him by the appropriate title in the proper setting, is great, but useless. It's the thing that prompted Jesus' response of, "*I never knew you, depart from me.*"

In a previous Chapter I talked about us being Ambassadors for Christ;

> 2 Corinthians 5:20 "*Now then we are ambassadors for Christ, as though God did beseech you by us: we pray you in Christ's stead, be ye reconciled to God.*"

I defined the function of an Ambassador as; "... ministers and representatives of a superior kingdom sent to a foreign one (in which we physically reside) to demonstrate the superiority of that heavenly kingdom in comparison to the rules, regulations, law, and principles of this earthly kingdom and those that rule over it ... choosing to practically demonstrate to the citizens of this realm the ascendant supremacy of our own, and the dominance of its benevolent sovereign head."

The manner in which we have understood and have been taught to demonstrate the superiority of that Kingdom has generally been limited to;

> *Matthew 10: 1, 7 and 8 "' (I give you) authority over unclean spirits, to cast them out, and to heal every disease and every affliction. 7 Say to them, The kingdom of heaven is at hand.' 8 Heal the sick, raise the dead, cleanse lepers, cast out demons. You received without paying; give without pay.*"

To say that this is the fullest extent of the demonstration of the superiority of the Kingdom in the Body of Christ is pathetic, for several reasons. The chief of them is that 98% of the church bought the lie that this sort of thing was limited to a few Apostles (the original 12) and that sort of thing is either not needed or unavailable to us today, or perhaps applies only to those who head a church. I can tell you from personal experience that those poor souls are part of the crew that preaches that stuff –or tells you to do it but never attempts it themselves.

To compound the error it has all been reduced to learning a few tools to evangelize (essentially invite people to church), forgive, don't smoke, don't drink, don't dance, no mixed bathing (swimming), don't, don't, don't, don't. None of which provokes anyone to jealousy … which by-the-way, has absolutely nothing to do with the instruction given in Matthew 10 above, or later in Matthew 28. The demonstration of the Kingdom of God is so much more than that.

If you will notice, throughout the New Testament Jesus never dealt with every demon He could see, feel or sense. He only dealt with the ones that stood between Him and what the Father had shown Him to do. In other words, Jesus was not distracted by every demonic manifestation that was presented to His eye, but He stayed fixed upon doing the job at hand, demonstrating that the Kingdom of God had come to town. He did not exclusively become a minister of deliverance, although He was one. So He was true to His mission in Life and the purpose He had for being here upon earth. Matthew 7:21-24 is an affirmation of that principle.

It is not enough to be able to cast out demons and heal the sick if there is no Kingdom purpose behind it because no element of the Kingdom will be established in the process. When the Lord said "I will establish (build) My church/" He obviously had a plan in mind and some steps that needed to be followed for that to happen. That's why He spent 3 and ½ years with 12 guys, whereupon He declared to them, *"If you've seen Me you've seen the Father."*

How many times have we seen people have their compassion and their emotions touched and decided that what touched them was the will of God for them. They sold everything, raised more funds and struck off on their own only to find their effort produced nothing – God wasn't in it.

The Kingdom is all about relationship; relationship with The Father, The Son, and Holy Spirit. If you look at the whole of the Bible, it is the story of God's relationship with a people that He chose. It's the ups and downs, the good, the bad and the ugly all laid out for us to see. Establishing and building the Kingdom is also an exercise in relationship.

Back in a previous Chapter, I related the story of God asking me "*What do you want?*" in connection with moving to Asheville, NC. Notice, I was ardently seeking His will, but He was also expanding my view of who He was and exposing me to another element of our relationship. The ins and outs of relationship are always a mystery until you're in it and the discovery process is continual. That's another element of Matthew 7:24. You have to stay engaged in it over time for you to really know someone. You have to be able to experience them in a variety of circumstances in order to get a decent picture of who they are and what motivates them, what they like and don't like.

Being raised as a Southern Baptist there wasn't much taught about a relationship with the Lord. It was primarily, get saved, get Baptized, read your Bible and be a good boy. The idea that you could actually get to know Go, like you could your friend or your spouse wasn't anywhere on the radar until I was around 34 years of age.

And I have to admit the concept was a bit scary because I'd read all those Bible stories about God opening up the ground and causing it to swallow 3,000 people, about Ananias and Sapphira (Acts 5) dropping dead for lying. Since we tend to get our original picture of who God is from our earthly fathers, mine was that of a stern, distant, aloof, demanding, authoritative God who would whip your butt for the slightest infraction. So I wasn't very keen on engaging Him one-on-one at first.

I am certainly glad I did or we would never have gotten to the *"What do you want?"* stage of our relationship. Just for your information, those events were about 17 years apart. There was quite a bit of water under the bridge between us during those years, and I can't say that I was the model son in that process either. And I'm still not where I want to be with Him either. But He's always been faithful to meet with me when I go to Him. And I think that's because of my history with my earthly father, and my early misconceptions of who He was. The Lord has always treated me gently, which I greatly appreciate.

So this begs the following questions;

- How connected are you to the Lord?
- How intimate is your relationship with Him?
- Do you know your purpose for being here on earth and know how it is to be expressed?
- Do you believe that you are walking in the center of the will of God for your life, or is there doubt?

22 Blessed To Be A Blessing

When Abraham was approached by God to enter into covenant with Him, His statement to Abram was 'you will be **blessed to be a blessing.**' When "Don't" is the sum total message of the church all that it is poised to generate is guilt and shame, which is a very poor motivator. The appearance of Kingdom people is supposed to create blessing, both for the people of the Kingdom and those they are in contact with. Guilt and shame is not a blessing, so there is something significant missing there.

Abraham was a wealthy man. If you are wealthy and you're supposed to be a blessing, then some of that wealth has to make it into the hands of those around you. You and I should be investors, not consumers; investing in our local economy, helping to fund new businesses, helping to educate, helping the poor to better their condition permanently, helping to heal and deliver.

A couple of years ago I was asked to do mock job interviews with a group of Senior High School students. I was stunned at how few of these kids had even sat down with an adult who had been around the block a few times to talk about their interests. I hope you caught the weight of that statement because what kids lack is life experience.

I was also surprised by how few of them could answer the question, "What do you want to do with your life?" I got several kids who answered, "I'm going to college" as though that was as far as they needed to think and that they would somehow magically be presented with all the options and they would figure it all out when they got there.

One kid was interested in doing something in athletics. He loved sports a great deal and played on both the football and basketball teams. His thought was that he was going to have to become an athletic trainer in order to stay around sporting activity. He had no idea that there are really only five colleges east of the Mississippi that had programs for athletic trainers and four of them were very expensive and entry is tough and very limited.

I spent a little while with him asking what kind of equipment either the school or the student-athlete had to buy in order to participate in just the two sports he participated in; socks, shoes, jocks, bags, balls, gloves, cleats, helmets, uniforms, pants and pads, mouth guards, sweatbands, athletic tape, knee braces ... and that was just the beginning. Next was how many other sports did his High School have available? He quickly rattled off half a dozen more.

Then I asked him about the local college. How many sports do they offer for men and women? The answer; football, baseball, basketball, soccer, field hockey, swimming, tennis, softball, wrestling, volleyball, golf, bowling, cross country, track and field (indoor and outdoor) and now they also have a bass fishing team. Every one of these sports has a totally different array of equipment. How many colleges are there in just this half of the state? Who sells all this stuff? How many people work for the athletic equipment manufacturers that supply all this stuff? Who are the distributors? How many coaches does that require? (Considering that track and field all by itself can have as many of fourteen different events in a single meet, there's a lot of individual sports equipment to be sold and that's just for the men's events.

I also told the kid that I knew a kid in Texas who turned filming High School football games into a career selling his wares to college coaches who were scouting potential recruits.

Then there was the story about us being in the golf business back in the mid 90's in the Atlanta, GA area and one of the guys who used to come in frequently was a sales representative for a major golf equipment manufacturer. We used to re-shaft drivers and fairway woods for him frequently. Over time we became friends. The equipment he sold was usually found at big box mass retailers, such as WalMart, Kmart, and Target stores. One day he invited us to his house for a birthday party. He gave us an address without directions. Well, to my great surprise MapQuest put his house in Country Club of the South, next to a mansion belonging to John Smoltz, a now hall of fame pitcher for the Atlanta Braves. Who knew there was that much money in low-end golf equipment? He must have been selling that stuff by the train load.

After just a few minutes this kid's whole world of possibilities in and around sports was blown wide open. And being an athletic trainer was just one of the lot. We didn't even talk about the manufacturing side of any of this multi-billion dollar industry.

My wife and I have spent a huge amount of time with the 20-somethings (singles and couples) in this community helping them to figure out how to do life. What to do next? How to deal with this problem, or fix that relational issue. Or in many cases, just a different view of the problem will give them sufficient clarity to handle it on their own. Plain ole mom and pop kind of stuff.

Some of these kids got stuck somewhere in the process, so we started a Saturday morning class for ten weeks that we called Life Launch - The Not-School. Thirty-two people signed up from age 19 to 72. We simply gave them a track to run on to help them figure out what they really wanted to do with their lives, and what road blocks they needed to deal with to get on with it. Then we offered them a couple of private sessions to deal with any issues holding them back from making a decision and actively engaging it.

Consequently, we've been part of encouraging young men and women in following their dreams and pursuing their goals. Part of that has been investing financially in the startup of a couple of local businesses that have made this little town a better place to live.

Part of that was to help the young turks figure out that they needed to invest in of their own time and energy in helping their friends succeed, which required them to go volunteer. Some of it involved free grunt labor. Some of it was passing out fliers, passing out free coffee as advertising, helping clean up, paint, or offering some skill that the future business owner didn't have to pay for. (One of the responsibilities of being in community.)

The key to life is giving yours away … and watching others be blessed by your gift and your experience. We are blessed to be a blessing and you can't be a blessing cooped up in your comfy little house sitting on the couch. You have to get out and rub shoulders with the folks who need what you have to give. You also won't experience being a blessing by writing a check. You may well become a blessing to someone by doing so, but if you really want to feel it you have to get out there and mix with them, get to know your neighbors and what they need to make life a little easier. Make your city a better, more friendly place to live. Be a blessing with your life and resources!

I hope I don't have to mention that section is taylor made for retirees or those soon to be. It also works well for those who are depressed about their current circumstance. Got involved with folks who have less than you do and you will find the atmosphere around will change dramatically.

23 Be A King In the Kingdom

The Old Testament life of King David is more than just a collection of stories about this young man who rose from back-woods obscurity to top of the heap. The life of David is also a picture of the church. As the chief ruler of Israel, he was a prophet, priest, and king. As believers, we know all about being priests before our God on behalf of others (or at least we should by now) and we are beginning to become more adept at it.

We are also becoming much more familiar with the prophets in our land, as well as the expression of the prophetic as a major demonstration of the Kingdom to unbelievers.

But thus far we are totally unfamiliar with the expression of Kingship in the Kingdom and how it relates to the conduct of our daily lives. I want to acquaint you with a couple of different expressions of it because we are going to see it rise steadily in the future, if you chose to notice.

First of all, who are Kings and what do they do? Living in a democracy (or so we've been told that's what this is) we are not readily familiar with their function and their authority. Kings are the highest authority in the kingdom. They rule and reign; meaning they make decisions and decrees that gets stuff done. They adjudicate disputes and determine what enterprise and practice are permissible and what is not. And their rule is law. So it was with King David. To aid him in reigning he sought counsel from several confidants and the local prophet of the Lord.

As part of the foundation of this idea on kingship, you need to understand and grab hold of the following revelation. The initiation of the ministry of Jesus was at His baptism by John. But there is a specific point in the narrative you need to be aware of ... because of the following verse, the Holy Spirit in the form of a dove (Matthew 3:16) did not rest upon the head of Jesus, but upon his shoulders ...

> Isaiah 9:6 *"For unto us a child is born, unto us a son is given: and* ***the government shall be upon his shoulder****: and his name shall be called Wonderful, Counselor, The mighty God, The everlasting Father, The Prince of Peace."*

> Isaiah 9:7 *"Of the **increase of his government** and peace there shall be no end, upon the throne of David, and upon his kingdom, to order it, and to establish it with judgment and with justice from henceforth even for ever. The zeal of the LORD of hosts will perform this."*

> Luke 1:33 *"And **he shall reign** over the house of Jacob for ever; and of his kingdom there shall be no end."*

The government of the Kingdom rests upon His shoulders. Since He (Jesus) is the head, and we are his body according to Ephesians 1:22-23, the government of the Kingdom rests upon you and me, working at the direction of the head.

Now for a little ancient history. This is precisely what Adam and Eve were charged to do in the Garden of Eden. They were told in Genesis 1:27 and 28 that,

> "And God blessed them. And God said to them, "Be fruitful and multiply and fill the earth and *subdue* it and have *dominion* ..."

Now I want you to take specific note of the two words in verse 28, _subdue_ and have _dominion_. What was on the earth that needed subduing and required it to be kept under the dominion of Adam and Eve? I can say with absolute certainty that it wasn't crabgrass. It had to be something a lot more significant than weeds to make it worthy of mentioning in scripture twice.

Earlier in history, we find that Lucifer decided that he wanted to be the big cheese instead of God. God obviously didn't think too much of his idea and booted he and his whole rebellious crew out of Heaven. The place they were thrown to was good ole planet earth. When he unceremoniously arrived, it was probably face first — at supersonic speed. After dusting himself off and feeling sorry for himself for a while, he became seriously angry; angry at God, angry at the angels that helped Him, angry at every human because were the height of His creation.

So the thing God was instructing man & woman to do when He created them was to take dominion over satan and his activities and to subdue him and his henchmen, thereby extending the atmosphere of the Garden as far as their dominion reached.

Subsequent to those days the devil's wrath has been taken out on people, by way of sin and wounds, trauma of varying types, generational iniquity and relational dysfunction. He took his anger out on the land God created through man's sin which has defiled the earth, and the recklessness which has polluted the earth's environment. The persistent use of powerful pesticides has found its way into our soil and water systems adding toxic chemicals to our food and water.Our thirst for energy consumption has further polluted the air and pour water. But most of all it has drawn a veil between us and heaven making it difficult for us all to connect and commune with the Lord.

Ephesians 2:1-3 _"And you were dead in the trespasses and sins_
**2** in which you once walked, following the course of this world,

*following the **prince of the power of the air**, the spirit that is now at work in the sons of disobedience 3 among whom we all once lived in the passions of our flesh, carrying out the desires of the body and the mind, and were by nature children of wrath, like the rest of mankind."* (ESV)

Since the enemy dominates the atmosphere it is our divinely given pleasure, birthright, and responsibility to take it back; to also cleanse and heal the earth of the defilement and restore it to the original blessing it was intended to be.

Psalms 149:4-9 *"For the LORD takes pleasure in his people; he adorns the humble with salvation.*
5 Let the godly exult in glory; let them sing for joy on their beds.
*6 Let the high praises of God be in their throats **and two-edged swords in their hands, 7 to execute vengeance on the nations and punishments on the peoples, 8 to bind their kings with chains and their nobles with fetters of iron, 9 to execute on them the judgment written**! This honor have all his godly ones. Praise the LORD!"*

Now if you still read this scripture with a mind that has been trained by the world, one that even now embraces the maxim that "might makes right," then you will no doubt conclude that we 'believers' are the world's peace keepers and punishers of all wrong-doers. Even though we might perhaps enjoy such a commission from on high, in thinking after that manner you will violate numerous other scriptures. Among them are ....

Ephesians 6:12 *"For we do not wrestle against flesh and blood, but against the rulers, against the authorities, against the cosmic powers over this present darkness, against the spiritual forces of evil in the heavenly places."*

Luke 6:27-28 *"But I say to you who hear, Love your enemies, do good to those who hate you, 28 bless those who curse you, pray for those who abuse you."*

Since you are primarily a spiritual being that has a soul (mind, will, and emotions) and lives in a body, we are obliged to fight the spiritual enemies that have ruled over this realm since they were booted out of Heaven.

I would refer you to our website www.houseofhealingministries.org/resources and look for a piece called *Angels and Demons*. This article delineates the spirits that are arrayed against us and helps us get a handle on where our authority in the name of Jesus, the name that is above every other name, begins and ends.

As Psalms 115 clearly states, *"The heavens are the LORD's heavens, but the earth he has given to the children of man"*

There is a limitation to the authority of man when it comes to dealing with higher order demonic beings. This article will help you understand where personal division line is.

At some point in the not too distant future we are going to see a shift in the functions of what we have understood as spiritual authority as we witness a few people morphing into temporary roles as kings. This will happen when the dividing line between good and evil is being so obliterated by the enemy that people will be calling evil good. We have seen good called evil and evil called good from time to time, but not like we will see it in the future as lawlessness becomes the order of the day.

It is beginning to be seen today with all the direct opposition inside and outside the government to the Presidency of Donald Trump. Twenty years ago this would have easily been considered treason. It is now considered by many to be the moral duty of those opposed to a man they didn't elect. The difficulty with this strategy is that what goes around also comes around. Our national government barely functions now. God help us in the future!

When that day arrives the Lord will speak to one of His children and tell them, even as he told prophets of old to go tell someone, "You have 48 hours to repent and stop doing what you are doing or you will die. I will pray for you that you will make the right decision." If they do not cease their evil, they will drop dead within the period specified. See the instance of Ananias and Sapphira in Acts 5:1-5, also King Nebuchadnezzar in Daniel 4. Imagine having to deliver that message to someone out of a heart of love.

Another element of this rising of the Godly men and women in the earth will be a significant, even violent opposition from the enemy through those sold out to him. Those declaring the judgment of the Lord will exercise it on leaders whose responsibility it is to lead a nation or a State righteously. It will not be a pronouncement upon masses of people.

Prior to these folks appearing from time to time we will see the establishment of city gate keepers. Generally, they will not be operating either under the auspices or in cooperation with local authorities as these may well not be righteous individuals. These folks will operate somewhat like Deborah did in Judges Chapter 4, independently of established religious and secular authorities. She regularly sat beside the highway between two significant cities helping their individual citizen solve problems and if asked, advising authorities regarding making decisions on behalf of many of their citizens. As a result of her work, she became a recognized authority in the region. Part of her function became determining by spiritual means what evil could not enter a city, what blessing could enter and what evil had to leave the city.

These individuals will operate in significant authority as protectors of cities, with the ability to determine what good and godly services prosper and which corrupt and inherently evil things fail and leave the city. They will be able to call for all local corruption to be exposed and it will be exposed.

This too will be a difficult task to remain in an attitude of love toward the offenders because God loves them in spite of their activities, despite the fact that their selfish actions often damage the lives of those we care about. (It's the free will thing.) Therefore we are going to have to allow the Lord of love to examine our hearts and grant us the grace to make the changes He desires to see in us. One cannot prepare for any of the previously noted assignments other than to love, for *"he who is faithful in little will be made ruler over much."* (Luke 6:10)

24 Forgiveness, et al

I haven't really wanted to place this extremely important element of the Kingdom among the last items in this book, for surely it is among the foremost characteristics to be demonstrated by Kingdom people. Scripture certainly has a great deal to say about it.

> Matthew 6:14-15 *"For if you forgive men their trespasses, your heavenly Father will also forgive you: 15 But if you forgive not men their trespasses, neither will your Father forgive your trespasses."*

> Mark 11:25 *"And when you stand praying, forgive, if you have ought against any: that your Father also which is in heaven may forgive you."*

> Romans 12:18 *"If it be possible, as much as it depends on you, live peaceably with all men."*

> Hebrews_12:14 *"Follow peace with all men, and holiness, without which no man shall see the Lord:"*

The bottom line here is that as Kingdom citizens we must live a life of forgiveness. Jesus stated a fact in John 16 that while we are about the business of the Kingdom in this world we will have ample opportunity to be offended, even persecuted (Matthew 13:21) because of our expression of the Kingdom and the declaration of the Word of the Lord. We must learn to live a life of forgiveness. How do you learn to do that? Practice! Simply gutting it out at each opportunity provided under the grace of the Lord; the subtle power of saying, Yes.

The world doesn't operate in that manner, in spite of the fact that every mental health professional understands that this is a necessity, but it is one of the foundational elements of all relationship and that's why the Lord is so insistent upon it. Not only in relationship with Him, but in relationship with each other.

It is patently obvious that this is the only manner in which to live in the context of marriage. You don't have to be married very long to come to the realization that it is something you can't live without; for we never marry someone like us and our differences present multiple opportunities for conflict. Failure to have it as one of the foundations of marriage is one of the chief reasons the divorce rate is slightly above 50%.

Sometime back I found myself in the place of dealing with a couple who had only been married 14 months, the last nine of which had been spent separated, living in two different cities. They decided to try and make a go of it and moved to the same city. They started attending the church we are a part of and asked if I could help them get back together.

I met with them three times. Each meeting turned into an uncontrollable argument. In the midst of their third "disagreement" in front of me, I abruptly called a halt to the proceedings and told each of them they had no other choice but to forgive each other or get a divorce. Then I told them, "Make your decision now! You have one minute!" I was interrupted twice before the minute was up with, "But, he/she did ..." at which point I repeated my demand, summing it up with "You have 30 seconds left. What's it gonna be?"

Neither of them said a word, nor did they look at one another. The time expired. I got up and said, "We're done here!" and turned off the light on my way out the door. They were divorced a few months later. If you're attitude is fixed on, "It's my way or the highway" you had better get used to walking through life alone.

Now don't misunderstand me, there are valid reasons for separation and divorce; infidelity, spousal abuse, criminal activity, repeated affairs and abuse of children. Chronic addictions (drug and alcohol) may on occasion be added to that list if it results in dangerous behavior that poses a threat to the spouse, the children or the neighbors. Failing to take out the trash, leaving dirty clothes on the floor and not being treated as you would like all the time are not included in that list.

We have a generation of emotional pansies who frequently use the phrase "that traumatized me or I was traumatized by ..." when all that really happened was that they got their feelings hurt. If that's you, you need to grow up and come to grips with the fact that life is often not fair and there is nothing you can do to make it that way. Trying to force others to live life and treat you like you want is a great prescription for personal misery and constant loneliness.

I will help anyone with their own personal baggage, but I don't do marriage counseling anymore. Primarily because by the time a couple feels the need to come to us for marriage counseling, it's much too late in the game to resurrect the relationship. If you are struggling in marriage please choose to find someone who will fight for the relationship, not simply become an ally to get your spouse to change into the person you want them to be. That will never work and you'll throw lots of money away in the process.

Here's another element of forgiveness that is absolutely necessary for each of us to be aware of. You cannot be offended because of something someone does to someone else. There is only grace to deal with your own wounds. There is none available for offenses that are not yours to resolve. Let me give you a couple of examples.

When one of your children does something you don't agree with to another of your children, like firing another family member from a business. Regardless of how wrong you think this is there are three facts you need to remember;

1) You don't know all the facts regardless of what the offended child says,

2) When a child gets hurt you automatically side with the one who got hurt and screams the loudest, and you therefore no longer have an objective viewpoint, and

3) Because of your closeness to those involved, you are no longer unbiased and are therefore are not in a position to resolve the squabble. And …

4) I repeat, there is only grace to deal with your own wounds and offenses. There is none available from God for wounds or offenses that are not yours. So don't pick up offenses that are not your own. There is absolutely no grace to carry it.

Here's another one. Your friend Bob makes a deal to buy a piece of property to build a house on from Roy, who is another friend of yours. As part of the sales agreement both men are to participate 50/50 (materials and labor) on building a fence to separate their two properties. For some reason Bob (the buyer) decides not to help build the fence, nor participate in the cost of the fence, reasoning that the purchase price should have included the fence's construction. Roy builds the fence and sends Bob a bill for half the materials, plus the wages for the laborer he had to hire to help him with the construction of the fence. Bob becomes angry and tells everyone who'll listen (folks who are also among your friends) that Roy is a jerk for treating him this way. Roy is offended and strikes back by telling everyone that knowing Bob's lack of integrity he should never have sold him anything and that he's ashamed to be living next to such a turkey.

Obviously, there were no witnesses to their agreement, so everyone is oblivious to the actual terms of the sales contract, or to the actual facts of what happened, but your friends start telling you (third hand) what Bob said and what Roy did wrong, and because they love Bob, they want you to get involved and help Bob get a fair deal.

Here are some iron clad facts you need to consider;

1) You don't know all the facts regardless of what the offended friends or their buddies have to say. Remember, there are always two side to every coin, even as there are to every story.

2) Since the info is at least 3rd hand (and none of your friends were personally involved) the chance that the truth might have been misheard, misunderstood, or stretched to generate sympathy by someone, is about 90%.

3) When a friend gets hurt we typically automatically side with the one who got hurt, which is the side year from first, and therefore you no longer have an objective viewpoint, and

4) Because of your lack of closeness to those involved, coupled with a lack of factual information, plus the fact that you are no longer unbiased, you are therefore not in a favorable position to help resolve the squabble.

5) You apparently have some pretty cowardly friends if they are coming to you to intervene in a squabble you have no responsibility to resolve. If they were true friends that would have tried to mediate the disagreement rather than trying to shanghais you into doing it.

6) I repeat, there is only grace to deal with your own wounds and offenses. There is none available for wounds or offenses that are not yours. So don't pick up offenses that are not your own, there is absolutely no grace to carry it, no matter how grievous it was. You cannot afford to get offended for someone else.

Someone is going to say, "Well what about righteous indignation. We certainly cannot tolerate someone running around terrorizing everyone in town." Unless someone elected you Sheriff, in which case you're limited to enforcing the existing laws, you have to quit judging others for what they do, or are thought to have done, or the reputation they supposedly have created that led up to this.

We have relocated to communities before where folks have told us negative things about "those people" and how they'll never be involved with them again, only to find out that "those people" were not exactly as despicable as we were told.

There is certainly room for discernment with people, but even then what you know (or think you know) should be kept to yourself, unless there is a real danger of harm involved. Generally, that's not the case. We have become so politically correct these days that someone getting their feelings hurt as a result of gossip is tantamount to a Federal offense.

I don't want to sound cold and heartless, but people need to grow up. Life is hard, it's unfair and it will never be the quiet, easy un-offended ride we hoped it would be. In many cases, people just need to toughen up a bit because their fragile egos are bound to get whacked frequently.

Forgiveness and Healing

Since I tend to deal with a large number of clients who are trauma victims, I find that the hardest ones to help heal are those who grew up in abusive environments, as well as those who grew up in homes with parents who were both angry, as well as, addicts. The environment of walking on eggshells and trying to be invisible is very damaging. The Lord gives us as children a natural love for our parents, so these folks never grew up consciously assigning blame to them. It's just the way things were, at least until as adults they came to the realization that their lives were currently as screwed up as their childhood was, and the hatred for their parents went all the way to the bone – yet was never acknowledged.

The key is still forgiveness, but it is a slightly different application. You see, forgiveness isn't, in and of itself, healing. You can't get healed without it, but forgiving the offenses won't get you healed all by itself. There is another step and it is the Isaiah 61:1 passage mentioning binding up the broken-hearted. For that is effectively what needs to happen where there was deep brokenness in the way children were raised. We are creatures that can only thrive on proper nurturing and healthy, wholesome attentiveness. Essentially, that means being raised by parents who are joyful in the parenting process. When that is not available, either by choice or brokenness, and we find this particularly in the homes of addicts, children must raise and care for themselves. We often see young children caring for the physical needs of their parents and their siblings as well, in spite of the fact that they should be being cared for.

Consequently, adult life is a long process of healing; figuring out how life really works as opposed to how they learned that it worked, unlearning their parent's attitudes, and prejudices, learning to trust again, learning appropriate responsibility when formerly they were responsible for everything, taking control of fear in all kinds of elements of life, along with creating a dependable, predictable normal for themselves.

As a result of living a life filled with fear there may also be other physical factors involved which can complicate the process like, fibromyalgia, chemical sensitivities, allergies and other auto-immune issues, chronic fatigue, hypersensitivity to sounds and situations, exaggerated fright responses and sleep disorders. Unfortunately, this cannot be healed when folks are all alone. It takes a support system comprised of prayer ministers, counselors, close friends, and supportive spouses. In short, a loving, comprehensive community that understands their issues, prays for them, supports them, helps them see their issues and responses accurately, and yet pushes them to be more than they currently feel they have the strength for. And it has to be a community that will stick with them for as long as it takes.

That community ought to be part of the church, but often it isn't. One reason that the broken often find themselves among a community of other broken people is that they are more accepting of others people's issues. And yet as comfortable as that may seem to be, it is also the least healthy environment they can be in and in many cases, it may actually retard their growth and healing.

While we lived in Asheville, NC we created a healing community that largely was the most complete one we've been introduced to. Every such community has its flaws but this one had very few. The hallmark of it was the caring hearts of its members who were more than willing to give of themselves when someone needed it. At its height, there were close to 50 people who were a part of it. There were many stories of financial gifts, of driving to meet someone at an odd hour to get a tire fixed, being a companion for a Doctor visit, hosting a birthday party, physical healings, taking someone to a movie or a dinner out, preparing meals for someone who was ill, helping people move, and on and on. We even took up a collection once and bought a woman a car.

The people came to us from great distances because an acquaintance of theirs told them that they got help here. And they came with every possible problem and issue you could name, including some we'd never heard of. They came for weeks on end, some of them for years. We had created or adopted programs for just about any presenting issue and highly trained and experienced people to carry them. It was a distinct honor and a privilege to be part of it.

It was a sanctuary for those who came to us as I believe every church ought to be. Sadly most are like clubs whose members gather once a week for a meeting to make them feel better about themselves, sort of a losers support group bound together by shame and duty. Just as sad, however, they are often not a safe, healing place for the broken and hurting because they have 'church' business to attend to. In all likelihood the reason they are not safe is that they don't, or won't, major in forgiveness.

I am not bashing churches, but I have attended more than few that were dead and lifeless because it was more about keeping up appearances than worshipping the risen savior and serving those He loved. Their pastors/rectors were only concerned with keeping everyone in the flock together so that they could continue to get paid and keep the building up. When 90% of the annual budget goes for little more than salaries, a mortgage, and operating expenses, it's time to re-examine the reason for its existence.

I'm off my soapbox now.

Forgiveness is an essential element of the demonstration that the Spirit of God dwells in you, that you are a disciple of Christ and your citizenship is in the Kingdom.

"Bless those who curse you." (Luke 6:8)

Judgment

If there is another significant tenet of the Kingdom life that we need to adhere to for the sake of the Kingdom it is not judging others.

> Romans 2:1-5 *"Therefore you have no excuse, O man, **every one of you who judges.** For in passing judgment on another you condemn yourself, because you, the judge, practice the very same things.*
> *2 We know that the judgment of God rightly falls on those who practice such things.*
> *3 Do you suppose, O man—you who judge those who practice such things and yet do them yourself—that you will escape the judgment of God?*
> *4 Or do you presume on the riches of his kindness and forbearance and patience, not knowing that God's kindness is meant to lead you to repentance?*
> *5 But because of your hard and impenitent hear,t **you are storing up wrath for yourself** on the day of wrath when God's righteous judgment will be revealed. "*

We are generally familiar with verse 1 of this passage but tend to skip over verses 3 through 5, which details a rather severe punishment for those who violate this commandment.

When Jesus was asked to declare what was the greatest commandment of all, He said,

> Matthew 22:37-40 *"And he said to him, "You shall love the Lord your God with all your heart and with all your soul and with all your mind.*
> *38 This is the great and first commandment.*
> *39 And a second is like it: You shall love your neighbor as yourself.*
> *40 On these two commandments depend all the Law and the Prophets."*

First of all, as humans, we are intimately familiar with all of our mistakes, our weaknesses, where we should have tried harder, planned better, done something different, or were downright wrongheaded about an issue and treated someone badly – in short, all of our failures. Our insecurities see to it that they are grossly magnified in our eyes. Consequently, we regularly choose to beat ourselves up over these trespasses, both great and small, even to the point of calling ourselves names and being abusive. This sort of behavior we consider to be quite normal, acceptable and even healthy in our performance oriented society. The world's system encourages us in it because it has taught it to us. We rationalize our agreement with it because it seems certain that it is a valuable exercise because none of us want to make the same mistakes over and over again.

However, we fail to recognize that this is a trap. As you and I get more mature we find that we become nicer and more tolerant of other people's mistakes and errors, failing to remember the admonition of Jesus Himself, **Love others as you love yourself** (verse 39).

Jesus is not happy when we treat others better than ourselves, particularly when it comes to self-flagellation following a mistake. We must break those ungodly habits and learn to be at least as kind to ourselves as we are to others.

I am not saying that we should live in denial regarding our behavioral habits. We all need to grow up and firmly address our childish ways. But when you continually berate yourself because you made a mistake you are secretly agreeing with the enemy that says, "There's actually something wrong with you. You need to try harder." That treadmill is specifically designed to kill you, so you need to get off before it does.

Secondly, our performance emphasis leads us to collect all kinds of personal rules and regulations that we choose to live by that we think will help us avoid failure, achieve success, and manage the risk of failure. The difficulty is that these rules and regulations are generally marks of perfection in life and we are at least for the time being, permanently human, unable to achieve perfection. Hence, we judge ourselves harshly for not being able to live up to the laws, rule, and regulations of our own making that we have amassed over the years that we hope will guarantee our emotional safety and progress in this world.

Not only do we judge ourselves in accord with these laws, but they are so good and so helpful that we judge everyone else by their ability to keep them as well, even if they have no idea that they exist. Our self-righteousness rule-keeping ways will always betrays us, for we tend to separate ourselves from those who refuse to keep the rules, law, and regulations we have so astutely acquired and apply to them. Herein we unknowingly fall victim to Roman 2:1-5 believing that we are doing it all for our own good, instead of finding that God is repulsed by it.

What we are experiencing in America, as well as the world over, is the fullness of the act of judgment itself as expressed in racism, a deep division between, races, sects, subsets of people, even on the basis of ideology. The deep divisiveness we see between Republicans and Democrats in the US during this most recent election cycle (Oct/Nov 2016) is a perfect example of this division. Neither trusts the other to even count ballots without chicanery – and this is in small towns among people who have lived happily next to one another for thirty to forty years.

The only thing one can say is that judgment is pure evil, which is why God's wrath is stored up for those who regularly practice it. Living by the letter of the law, even if it is of your own making, will kill love in you for others, which is actively a violation of another of His commands. Living life by the laws we create means we are striving to live life out of our heads by measuring everything for its potential to harm us, in hope that can avoid every possible snare. When you have to live life from your head you can't live it from your heart, which is the most creative part of you.

As a human, I will never be perfect. I will mess up more often than I'd like, so avoiding failure is impossible. So living by my own set of laws means I will violate one or more of them more often than not. That brings fear. And that begets more rules to follow to fight it. My failures usher in shame, and when shame gangs up on you, depression will not be far behind.

As Kingdom citizens we must allow God to search our hearts for any shred of living life by the law, and the unforgiveness that it generates in us. For in living life by the law we cannot live life by the Spirit, which is how we were created to live. This will allow Holy Spirit to convict us of sin and convince us of the virtue and blessing of righteousness in each area of our lives. Otherwise, we risk becoming outcasts from the Kingdom at worst, and the very least in the Kingdom of God, at best.

Another Element of Kingdom Life

Recently we received a letter from an individual who is also in ministry making a serious accusation. Frankly, the letter hurt. Why the individual couldn't pick up the phone to see if we could sort this out was part of the hurt. The other part was hurtful was in this individual's struggle to quantify, understand or validate the accusations he was considering there were apparently several conversations held with other ministers about this situation. After sitting with the Lord for a couple of days the answer was to go low, in spite of how I felt about the whole affair.

There are occasions when stuff happens that you have a choice to make – and you do have a choice. You can either choose to let the situation ruffle all your feathers and raise a stink, or you can take a deep breath, give it to God and do what needs to be done to make peace and to keep your peace. When situations like this arise our sense of justice, or right and wrong, is perverted by the offense we choose to take, and in doing so we fall squarely into the trap the enemy has laid for all parties concerned. There are plenty of battles that are not your to fight and if you will learn to find out which ones fall into that category life can be much more enjoyable.

25 Kingdom Authority

The following is an excerpt from another book of mine (available on Amazon.com) entitled *Angels and Demons*. The full book scripturally lays out the names of and the authoritative hierarchy of the demonic entities that are arrayed against us and proposes a question each of us must engage as Kingdom dwellers. We have been told that we have been given authority over spiritually launched attacks against us and those we have been assigned to protect in the mighty name of Jesus, the name that is above every other name. Sometimes it works and sometimes it doesn't. What's the deal? Where does my spiritual authority begin and end? Why does it work sometimes and not at others?

The point of it is that there are strategies launched against us by much higher order demonic beings that are enforced or enacted by numerous lower order demonic beings. These strategies are planned against us due to;

a) our individual personal God-given Kingdom assignment here on earth, or

b) our connection or relationship to others who's assignments are significant to the Kingdom, or

c) our part in specific plans to establish specific elements of the Kingdom of God here on earth that are both time and location sensitive and

d) against our ability to search the Halls of Heaven for real solutions to the problems we are experiencing here on earth.

So where is the demarcation line between what we have to ask God to deal with and what we have the authority over in the name of Jesus and the responsibility to deal with here on earth in the name of Jesus?

I propose two answers to this question. The first is rooted in two scriptures;

Colossians 2:15 "*And having spoiled principalities and power, he made a show of them openly, triumphing over them in it.*"

Ephesians 3:10 "*To the intent that now unto the principalities and powers in heavenly places might be known by the church the manifold wisdom of God,*"

These two verses would tend to indicate that the line is right at or slightly below these two named authorities. As a much younger believer who tried to take on a principality single-handedly, I can tell you that I bear the scars from having done so, with no apparent damage done for all the effort. So when in doubt about where the limits of personal authority lay, it's always a safe bet to simply ask the Lord to deal with them. (It's worked well so far.)

Secondly, what I've come to understand is that it's not the same for everybody. Each of us has different Kingdom assignments. And some of those assignments even have seasons appointed for them. Each of us also has different responsibilities, realms of influence and authority and each of us is situated in different geographical areas that possess holy items, or territory, or formerly holy things that have been taken over by the enemy that the Lord wants to be redeemed. Each of us has varying levels of faith and a different array of gifts. Each of us has also been sent to a different "tribe" of people, socio-economic group, etc. Also, just as in the early years of the New Testament, there are different positions in the body; (Ephesians 4) apostles, prophets, evangelists, pastors, teachers, elder, and deacons; these individuals were both given authority in the name of Jesus to do specific things, but also tasked with earning increased authority to do other things. So it is with us 2000+ years later.

Further, each of us has reacted differently to the challenges of life that we've faced, which is how we develop character and gain authority ... or not. Some of those reactions resulted in increasing maturity and some resulted in having to take the test again. Have you ever come to the conclusion that as wonderful as life is without problems, we never grow or learn anything during the peaceful times? It's only through the difficult times that we learn and make progress. That's when authority is gained. (See James Chapter 2) The depth of the struggle and our weakness during tough times is responsible on occasion for our choice to live in denial about an issue, or worse yet, recognize the issue but act like a turtle and pull our head inside our personal shell of emotional safety to wait out the storm – no authority gained.

So perhaps the question could be more aptly put as ... Where is that dividing line for you?

Since we evangelicals are always keyed in on the bad guys and have therefore given them much more press than they deserve, I would like to spend a few moments extolling the virtues of engaging life and ministry with the Godly entities (we seem satisfied to ignore) in the Kingdom as an integral part of the efforts we are involved in.

As you may recall, there were only one-third of the existing angels that fell with Lucifer – leaving twice as many spiritual good guys as there were bad guys. And it wasn't just the tough ones that bailed on God. It was the arrogant stupid ones.

I would also remind you of the following; Hebrews 1:13-14

"But to which of the angels said he (God) at any time, Sit on my right hand, until I make your enemies your footstool? 14 **Are they not all ministering spirits, sent forth to minister for them who shall be heirs (you) of salvation?**

Next time you need help just ask them to come to your aid. You'll find that they are quite handy to have around.

Switching gears ...

You may want to remember verse 15,

Colossians 2:13-15 *"And you, being dead in your sins and the uncircumcision of your flesh, hath he quickened together with him, having forgiven you all trespasses;*
14 Blotting out the handwriting of ordinances that was against us, which was contrary to us, and took it out of the way, nailing it to his cross;
15 **And having spoiled principalities and powers, he made a show of them openly, triumphing over them in it.***"*

The definition of "spoil" according to Webster's 1833 Dictionary is,

1. To plunder; to strip by violence; to rob; 2. To seize by violence; to take by force; as, to spoil ones goods. 4. To corrupt; to vitiate; to mar. 5. To ruin; to destroy. 6. To render useless by injury 7. To injure fatally.

In other words, Jesus stripped the enemy of ALL of his weapons. The only ones he has remaining are deception and lies ... and of course death, the last enemy.

I know many of you say that this is NOT true because you have been made ill, suffered loss, been used and abused, betrayed, had accidents and injuries and suffered (or are still suffering) with such things as fibromyalgia, arthritis, adrenal failure, insomnia, chemical sensitivities and food allergies through no fault of your own – you suffered an unprovoked attacked.

I would agree, yes, the enemy did indeed bring these things. God did not. But there is this little verse in the Old Testament found in Proverbs 26:2

> "As the bird by wandering, as the swallow by flying, so the curse causeless shall not come." (KJV)

That means that for the overwhelmingly vast majority of the earth's population there is a valid reason that you are, or have suffered these things. There are several possibilities;

1. Your own personal behavior; fears, unforgiveness, control, judgments, lack of self-control, attitudes, greed and avarice, jealousy, lust, anger, dependencies and other addictions, dysfunctional or destructive personal habits, etc.
2. Family baggage and generational curses.
3. Demonic assignments against you by enemies and occult practitioners.
4. Retaliation by the enemy in response to taking his territory, personal or corporate.
5. Living on defiled ground or inhabiting defiled property.
6. Living in a polluted fallen world.

Many of you reading this Chapter have already freaked out because neither abuse, nor trauma (physical, spiritual or emotional), including accidents, were specifically mentioned wherein you undeservedly suffered injury inflicted upon you. Your case falls in line with a combination of numbers 1 and 3. Ultimately, it is our response to numbers 3 through 6, including abuse and trauma inflicted intentionally or otherwise, that creates our pain and discomfort. What we did or didn't do with that pain makes a significant difference. Perhaps we didn't know how to get to God to get healed, or never knew we needed it because of our lack of self-awareness, or our propensity to live in denial, childhood dissociative strategies or deeply suppressed memories until you were well into adulthood. It is still our own personal responses and behaviors that resulted in most of our afflictions that created these problems because no one taught us what to do. I fully understand that none of these was your fault, however, it is always our non-redemptive default response strategies for self-protection that actually produces the damage.

So when we talk about Kingdom Authority and exercising it in our fallen world, we have to begin with ourselves by putting the Lord back in the place He belongs rather than continuing to suffer under the ministry of the demonic buggers that have made our existence troublesome. A couple of the methodologies I have personally employed to make that happen are covered in three of the books I have written.

The first of these was a book entitled, "*Defeating Jezebel*." (Available on Amazon) In it I describe a technique taught to us to defeat the attack of a bunch of lower order demonic entities initiated by Jezebel. This sort of thing is quite common in the Body of Christ because we live in a part of the World that this spirit is over. Its attack against us is so sly, so sneaky, so subtle, that most people don't know it's actually happening until the full weight of it is about to suffocate them. It teaches you who your enemy is, How to recognize them and how to neutralize the attack and get back under the fountain of the Lord's grace.

The second book is entitled "*The Effects of Trauma and How to Deal With It*" and is (the 3rd Edition) also available from Amazon.

Recovering from any traumatic situation, whether it a physical injury, or a highly emotional wounding, or both, is very difficult because the effect of it impacts our entire being, physically, emotionally and spiritually. If you do not deal with the spiritual impact first, then the recovery process is not only lengthened, but it also becomes torturous; the tormenting dreams, the flashbacks, the disturbed sleep, the easily touched trigger mechanisms, etc. This prayer tool helps you deal with it and allows you to help others as well.

The third book is entitled "*The Insidious Dance, The Paralysis of Perfectionism*" also available from Amazon. This book addresses the problems we struggle with having grown up in a world where what we do and how much we do declares our personal value and importance in this world. It reveals the specific symptoms that many of us have had to wrestle with and provides us with a method to escape its iron grasp.

I have given you a few hints at some of the things I've personally had to deal with through the three previous paragraphs and in a couple of previous Chapters. I have found over the previous 35 years that perhaps the most consistently helpful thing has been going to people periodically to minister to me. Some of you are thinking, 'What the heck does that have to do with exercising your Kingdom authority?' If you cannot resolve the issues yourself, or just between you and God, then go and get help – let them exercise Kingdom authority on your behalf. In essence, deputize them to bring order where you can't do it on your own. That is another means of establishing your authority, by simply giving it to someone else qualified to help you. It often takes an unbiased view of things to help us see things as they really are rather than what I have always presumed them to be.

Let me give you another personal example. My wife and I have agreed that we will go for personal ministry every two years or so. Well, in the middle of January we were overdue by about five years. So I trooped down to the Nashville, TN area for an all-day session with a couple of gracious prayer ministers I had been introduced to.

As the session began the lead said, "You're a father!" I replied, "Yes, I know. But there was a time I didn't want that title because I felt that it would make me responsible for people – people I didn't even like." To me it was just an off-handed response to her statement of something I already knew. But to her there was something in it that had to do with what the Lord wanted to deal with that day, and that's what she went after. The discernment of those around us is often able to know or see things you and I never will. It's why we need each other so much.

In the early going of the session Jesus kept flipping five or six small keys up and down lightly in His hand. I asked Him what they were. He said these are the keys to your heart, the places that you have reserved for yourself to keep out the additional pain. I asked Him what the largest of them was to. Instantly I had a memory of a situation that occurred about 20 years ago. Pat had kept asking me to protect her. Will you just protect me! I need you to protect me! My response was, "From What?" To my knowledge there was no one stalking her, no one coming after her. There was no one attacking her. As far as I knew, she was in no danger whatsoever.

That's when it hit me. There was evidently a part of my heart that I had kept from her that somehow made her feel unsafe. People are spiritually sensitive to their mates, and this is particularly true more-so for women than for men. She could never put her finger on it but she somehow knew she didn't have all of me and that made her feel unprotected.

When we build protective walls around portions of our heart to protect ourselves from additional hurt, those walls are indiscriminate about what they keep out. They even keep out the very love you want and desperately need. They not only block the fullness of relationship with a spouse, but anybody else as well, including the Lord.

I mention this experience because there is no way I would have ever been able to get there by myself. I needed these two gals to guide me into it and then their guidance to discover and work through all the lies and half-truths that were wrapped up in the initial event that caused me to respond the way I did in the first place. That's why there has to be some level of trust that you and I walk in that allows us to go to people and dare to tell them what we are struggling with. We need each other. Remember, No man is an island.

As we wade through the obstacles that stand in our way of exercising the Kingdom authority we've been given individually, the Lord often provides us with frequent opportunities to grow in exercising it in behalf of others. In this process we are forced to deal with our issues of doubt and unbelief, as well as our pride and prejudice that will not allow us to have compassion for others who are struggling. Several years ago we started a set of healing rooms in the church we were in near Asheville, NC. That provided the perfect environment to exercise our faith that God would show up in other people's health issues and family situations as we asked God to move on their behalf. I have often described it like this; the perfect place to look like an idiot if God never chooses to show up.

That statement simply expressed what I have always felt. There needs to be some intentionality in the expression of our Kingdom authority. It has been delivered to each of us. We just don't have any confidence (faith) that anything will happen if we exercise it because we have never exercised it over any length of time to find out.

Most long-term trauma sufferers I have known commonly exhibit a similar issue; they are angry with God because he never answered their prayers for deliverance from their mental anguish, or physical and emotional pain. I wish there were an easy answer for them that didn't require living in, and struggling through, community and choosing to blindly trust God and people, despite what they've suffered. There will be no relief until some measure of it is risked.

The same is true for each of us when it comes to praying for others. Yes, the fact is that God could choose not to show up in response to our prayers, but for whatever reason He has sovereignly chosen to both create man, and to create him in a manner that He could use him to do His bidding here on earth. That alone tells me that He wants to answer our prayers on behalf of others ... and ourselves. We simply have to put ourselves in a position to pray for more people. In the seven-plus years we operated those healing rooms we saw all manner of miracles, including some marvelous things that you and I would not consider miraculous, but were so valuable to those who came.

One such story was of a short little old lady who dressed very properly even in warm weather. A stylish long gray coat, sensible black pumps, a shiny black purse hung smartly from right her arm, thick black framed glasses, and her spotless white gloves. She drove some sort of lumbering giant of a car, a 20-year-old, gray 4 door to see us each week. Her diminutive height would only allow her to view the road from between the dashboard and the steering wheel, with her gloved hands completing the frame. Quite a sight if you were walking through the parking lot when she arrived. She caused you to quicken your pace when she rolled in.

She would come promptly 15 minutes after we opened. She would sit quietly awaiting her turn to enter one of the prayer rooms. When her name was called she came in and sat down, put her purse down beside her, removed her gloves and folded her hands in her lap. It was always the same thing she came in for every week; prayer for healing of her arthritic neck and recovery of her sight due to macular degeneration. Nothing more!

Well, I don't know about you but I am a firm believer in touching people as I pray. Some would use the old-fashioned term 'the laying on of hands.' So one or more of us would put a hand on her shoulder and pray up a storm, then bless her, give her a round of hugs and send her home. After one such evening, about the 40th in a row, I asked the Lord, "Why does she continue to come? There's been no change." He quickly said, "This is the only place she gets touched by another human being all week long, and she needs it so badly."

In the eyes of the Lord that was time well spent each week. Even if she were the only one who came each week it was worth it by His value system.

We were her community. Such is His Kingdom.

One Last Word

Jesus said in John 10 that He came that you might have life, and life abundant. Certainly destiny and purpose being fulfilled is all about life. But, there is more to life than doing the works that were established for us to perform before the foundation of the world. Life is all about relationship.

In Matthew 19, Jesus is asked by a young, performance-oriented, rich guy what else he needs to check off his list of things to do in order to achieve eternal life. Jesus slaps him upside the head with his retort of, "*Well … if you would enter into life, keep all these commandments …(v.17).*" All the commandments Jesus gave him were not about what not to do (don't lie, don't steal, don't covet), they were the foundational elements of basic relationships, that is, how you treat your neighbors, your employees, your fellow synagogue attendees, etc. In other words, Jesus was saying that one of the chief ways of insuring that you are qualified to enter the Kingdom of Heaven is to be certain you qualify as a good friend, a neighbor, a son, a brother or a sister.

How you live before God is seen in how you live before men and vice versa.

God is really into personal relationships. Why else would he say in Matthew 5:23 that if you're in church and you remember that somebody has something against you, leave and go make it right? Or, in Matthew 6:14-15, that if you want forgiveness from God, you have to forgive.

Some time ago we had a series of young people come through our office door expressing that they were frustrated that life seemed to be passing them by. They were afraid that they were missing their destiny. I assured them that it was not at all likely that they would miss what God had for them. But just to make sure, I began a word study on the word "destiny" in scripture. What I found was surprising. There is only one verse in the New Testament translated as "destiny" and it declares that we are "destined" to become conformed to the image of Jesus Christ (Romans 8:29). When I looked at the meaning of destiny, I was even more surprised because that word carries with it the connotation of fate. In other words, being conformed to the image of Christ is going to happen.

A single verse with reference to destiny and then, by contrast, the balance of the New Testament was written entirely about relationship. It ought to be apparent to us that relationships are the key to real life, but somehow we still prize independence and eschew connectedness. For most of us, it is the pain of trauma, derived from those whom we were supposed to be able to trust, thrust upon us, which has left us unable to trust and enter fully into healthy relationships. Conversely, it is through healthy relationships that we will recover our identity and experience the abundant life of joy-filled, meaningful relationships. Such is the Kingdom of God.

26 Kingdom Habits

Obviously there are some habits that as Kingdom men and women we need to create if we are to become and remain Kingdom minded. Failure to do so will jeopardize our ability operate as Kingdom Ambassadors as we should. I am not going to expound at length on each one because as a believer you should know them and be practicing them on some level already. But in case you are not doing so already, here's my list.

- **Reading your Bible** at least every other day, including systematic study. Do not read your Bible for information. Don't read it as information to be passed on to those who need it. That is not relationship. The world values information. Read it for insight into God's character and what He is saying to you through it. Read it for what it says to you. Get to know Him through it. That's actually the reason why He had it written.
- **Frequent private worship times.** Scripture tells us that God inhabits the praises of His people. So if you are looking for the presence of God in your life you have a promise to hold onto. I find that many people who engage in corporate worship don't really know how to worship, because they don't really know what worship is not how to conduct it. They become self conscious and get distracted too easily. If you are not intentional about worshipping in private, then whenever the public opportunity arises, you will not be able to enter in.
- **Scheduled periods of solitude** for meditation and reflection on the Word. Our schedules are way too busy and we think if we're

not busy we are not productive. Being continually busy is a sure fire way to lose yourself and your way in life. Try to take a sabbatical periodically, a two or three day every six months, or a spiritual retreat for five days once a year by yourself. Solitude is not the same as loneliness. Yes, you are by yourself, but you have to remember that the Holy Spirit of God dwells within you and He is able to nurture, comfort, heal, teach, bring wisdom and help discover the hidden motivations of the heart that keep you from being the best version of yourself you can be. You cannot access all that He has to offer being busy.

- **Do not despise other people's pain**. Get close to and be there for those who are struggling. You and I were made for love and relationship. Distancing yourself from the hurting because you feel unprepared or can't be bothered because these folks are too needy says more about your spiritual condition than you realize. If you can't handle other people's pain then connect with people who know how to do what you can't and learn from them. Remember, Jesus didn't come for those who had it all together. He came for the hurting, the broken, the down trodden, the widows and the orphans – those who could not help themselves. You and I were created in His image, which says we have to be engaged with those same folks.

- **Daily Journaling**: this is a two pronged effort with one being a frequent exercise in journaling what you feel, what you think and where you are struggling. This will help you be more self aware and honest about where you are emotionally. It's the process of becoming aware of the hidden motivations of your heart. The second element should include frequently journaling what God is saying to you (intentional listening. Often times we go to God in prayer and never stop to listen because we are so intent on telling our side of the story and fail to give god the opportunity to speak into those situations. He is not only the

God of information, but He's also the source of all comfort and you can't receive it if you are talking all the time.

- **Obedience**: The following is a recent FB post of a young man from Canada that I met at IRIS Global's Harvest School in Pemba, Mozambique a couple of years ago that speaks to a major discipline needed in the lives of every Kingdom subject.

"It was month two of being home from Mozambique when Papa God poised this question to me. "*Do you know what is the most difficult thing that God-followers have struggled with from the beginning of creation*?" I took 5 minutes trying to think of something other than the all in-compassing response of, "sin". Unable to come up with what it could be, He finally stepped in at my request and answered with this one word------ "Obedience."

Obedience? Really? Then it clicked!

All throughout history man has failed in obeying the Almighty's commands! Then He said to me, "*If you do not learn obedience in the smallest of commands, Stephen, how can you know Me more fully? How can you fulfill your destiny that I have spoken over you? How can you avoid the pitfalls of the saints before you*?"

In response to that conversation, I have spent the last 17 months trying to obey His smallest of commands.... and I can tell you honestly, that it has been the hardest thing I have ever tried to do! My mentality was raked to roots of its stability! My intellect was brought down (to) bedrock! My trust in my personhood was shattered.... If I said that the last 17 months have been THE HARDEST I have ever lived through in my 24 years, it would be a gross understatement! More than a dozen times I yelled at God to go find someone else to fulfill His commands! Go touch someone else!!! And yet, I could not back up my words and walk away ---- for this one reason. Every day He would show up in a love that was like the intensity of fire itself! If I allowed him to speak but for a few minutes, I would fall head over heels in love with Him again! Song of Solomon doesn't come CLOSE in describing the pure, holy, unaltered love of the Divine!!! I would struggle some times for weeks on end, arguing with Him, blaming and accusing Him, and yet, I could not deny the rights ------ of holy love ------ when He would draw near and whisper, "Stephen." "I love you.""

If you are not struggling with obedience then you have made Christianity all about you. And in your freedom you are denying the claim He has on you because of the profession of faith you made when you first met Him. There is no Kingdom without a King and His subjects do what He says or they are merely imposters walking in self delusion about their Kingdom status.

Not sure when this was originally published, but it runs hand-in-hand with the above:

He is Coming to You as Fire!

Have you ever prayed, "Lord, show Me Your glory?" Or have you asked for more of God's fire?

There are times when God comes softly, and there are times He comes as *Fire*. And I believe now is one of those times, for many of us who have been hungering for Him, this is a time when He says:

"Beloved, this is what you asked for, when you earnestly desired Me and craved My glory and brightness. You called for My fire."

And you see Jesus as you have never seen Him before. The Apostle John was stunned, as he encountered Him like this:

"The hair on His head was white like wool, as white as snow, and His eyes were like blazing fire. His feet were like bronze glowing in a furnace...His face was like the sun shining in all its brilliance." (Rev. 1:14, 16, NIV)

What Does Love Look Like?

Because God loves you and because He values you as a priceless treasure—more than gold, silver or precious jewels—there are times when He will draw near to you with His fire. God's fire speaks of His presence and His glory...His love, His holiness. Fire speaks of Who He is. *"Our God is a consuming fire"* (*Heb. 12:29*).

> The Prophet Malachi wrote: *"But who will be able to endure it when He comes? Who will be able to stand and face Him when He appears? For He will be like a blazing fire that refines metal, or like a strong soap that bleaches clothes. He will sit like a refiner of silver, burning away the dross. He will purify the Levites, refining them like gold and silver, so that they may once again offer acceptable sacrifices to the Lord."* (*Mal. 3:2-3*, NLT)

To love God is to honor and welcome Him as the One Who is many things to us. He is Saviour, Healer, Shepherd, King, Prince of Peace, and He is also Consuming Fire. In this moment of revelation, we have a choice. Will we give Him the desire of His heart, or draw back? Will we yield to the temptation to keep something from His holiness?

Because His fire scorches that which is unholy. The fire of His holiness consumes sin and self-will, but offers in its place, wealth beyond imagining as you have intimacy with the Beloved! Oh, how He wants you!

> *"Place me like a seal over Your heart, like a seal on Your arm; for love is as strong as death, its jealousy unyielding as the grave. It burns like blazing fire, like a mighty flame."* (*Song of Songs 8:6* NIV)

The Invitation

There is a choice...one Jesus will not make on our behalf. It is a decision only we can make.

> "In a large house there are articles not only of gold and silver, but also of wood and clay; some are for special purposes and some for common use. Those who cleanse themselves...will be instruments for special purposes, made holy, useful to the Master and prepared to do any good work." (2 Tim. 2:20-21, NIV)

For "those who cleanse themselves" this is an opportunity to make an offering of your all to Him—to present yourself to His fire, which yields unlimited possibilities.

It is time for consecration:
• To dedicate your heart, mind, body and whole life to Him.
• To allow the Holy Spirit to put His finger on whatever aspect of your life and your will He pleases and to bring adjustment.
• Gently, and yet relentlessly, your Father reveals the work that needs to be done.
• It is His offer of supreme grace.
In that place of raw honesty, where nothing hides, you yield the soul attitudes that have dampened your joy and the pain and that history to Him. In His love, He pulls you into His fire and His purging flame burns up what is not of Him. Mercy prevails, removing all shame. You discover a greater intimacy with Him than you have known before.

The Fire Burns in You

Jesus speaks to His lukewarm Church, echoing the Words of the Prophet Malachi, "For He will be like a refiner's fire or a launderer's soap." (see Mal. 3:2-3). He will say,

"I counsel you to buy from Me gold refined in the fire, so you can become rich; and white clothes to wear, so you can cover your shameful nakedness; and salve to put on your eyes, so you can see" (Revelation 3:18, NIV).

As we respond, He purges, He fills, He replenishes. The fire that cleanses the impurities now causes the vessel—you—to glow with a heavenly brightness. The same fire that removes what has bound you, now burns in you. It is a fire of His holiness. What once hurt and defiled you, has been removed. And in its place, you contain the fire of His bright, glorious presence. You know the touch of the Master.

My Prayer: *Father, I know Your call is going out. And I ask for those whose hearts resonate, who say 'Yes!' to You—who have asked for You to come with fire and who have perhaps, up until now, not known what they have asked for. And they are catching a glimpse. Come, by Your Spirit and make them brave.*

Helen Calder, Melbourne, Australia   Email: helen@enlivenpublishing.com

Made in the USA
Columbia, SC
22 August 2018